THE HOSTA BOOK

THE HOSTA BOOK

by
Paul Aden

with
Dr. Lillian Eichelberger Cannon
John Elsley
Harold Epstein
Nora Fields
Mabel Maria Herweg
Yoshimichi Hirose
Dr. Samuel B. Jones, Jr.
Graham Stuart Thomas
Andre Viette

CHRISTOPHER HELM
London

ISBN 0-88192-087-8
Printed in Singapore

Timber Press
9999 SW Wilshire
Portland, Oregon 97225

Library of Congress Cataloging-in-Publication Data

Aden, Paul.
    The hosta book : making sense of gardening / by Paul Aden with
Lillian Eichelberger Cannon ... [et al.].
        p.   cm.
    Includes index.
    ISBN 0-88192-087-8 : $29.95
    1. Hosta.   I. Title.
SB413.H73A34 1987
635.9'34324--dc19   87-26733
                                                         CIP

First published in Great Britain in 1988 by
Christopher Helm (Publishers) Ltd, Imperial House,
21-25 North Street, Bromley, Kent BR1 1SD

ISBN 0-7470-0006-9

Contents

About the Contributors

Graham Stuart Thomas Considered by many as the world's leading gardening writer. His books include: *Perennial Garden Plants,* and *The Art of Planting.* He has been awarded the O.B.E., V.M.H., D.H.M., and V.M.M., and is currently Gardens Consultant to the National Trust, England.

Andre Viette Highly respected author and lecturer; teaches several horticultural courses; recipient of many distinguished awards; owns a leading nursery which grows over 3,000 varieties of herbaceous perennials.

John Elsley Could be described as a "plant-hunter," lecturer; travels worldwide to search out promising new plants for Wayside Gardens and George W. Park Seed Company; radio and television appearances. Formerly botanist at the Royal Horticultural Society, Wisley Gardens; and curator of hardy plants at the Missouri Botanic Garden.

Dr. Lillian Eichelberger Cannon A medical researcher with an extensive list of scientific papers to her credit. An avid and knowledgeable gardener, she has written about what she owns and grows.

Harold Epstein Lecturer, author, editor, recipient of many distinguished service awards; has led horticultural travel groups for decades; has introduced many plants to North America from abroad; a long horticultural involvement, including President Emeritus of American Rock Garden Society.

Mabel Maria Herweg Experienced teacher of Japanese, Chinese and American flower-arranging at Arnold Arboretum, University of Rhode Island, Massachusetts Horticultural Society etc.; has spent years studying the art of Ikebana, Japanese flower arrangement and garden design in Japan; author of many articles on flower-arranging.

Nora Fields Noted lecturer and author on flower-arranging; headed flower-arranging program at the New York Botanical Garden; clients include many leading corporations.

Yoshimichi Hirose Co-author of the definitive book on plant variegation, *Variegated Plants,* as well as numerous books and articles; extensive lecture and television appearances; currently, a horticultural consultant on succulents for arboreta and landscape architects.

Dr. Samuel B. Jones, Jr. Botanist at the University of Georgia; author of many scientific books; currently involved in extensive research on hostas.

Paul Aden Compiler and editor; landscape designer and consultant; author of many magazine articles; recipient of many distinguished awards; lectures, conducts workshops and seeks new plants internationally; radio and television appearances; specialty is variegated, "easy-care" landscape plants; currently, working as consultant in developing and marketing new plants for the leading perennial nurseries.

Special Acknowledgements

Aside from the special writings of the contributors, this book owes much to other persons. With the book "in progress" over a period of fifteen years, the cumulative judgements and support of my family, namely my wife Estelle, and my daughters Victoria J. and Amy J. Aden certainly eased the way. Mr. Richard Abel, of Timber Press, with his incisive judgements of gardener's needs, along with Mr. Roy Klehm, of the Klehm Nursery, with his faith in the genus and his general support of education for the gardening public that would demonstrate the variety of uses of hostas, helped mightily. Tom Everett and Carl Totemeier of New York Botanical Garden, as well as Gordon Jones of Planting Fields Arboretum were most helpful, as was Mr. C. D. Brickell, Director General of the Royal Horticultural Society and John Bond of Savill Gardens. Nurserypersons, such as Beth Chatto, of UNUSUAL PLANTS and Alan Bloom of BRESSINGHAM NURSERIES gave freely of their time in discussing and evaluating tracts of the book, as was Mr. M. KAMO of KAMO NURSERIES in Japan. Protracted conversations with Dr. Fumio Maekawa, Dr. Noboru Fujita, Dr. Shu Hirao, Dr. Y. Tsukamoto and Dr. Masuto Yokoi all helped mightily. Valuable input and support was also received from Dr. Warren I. Pollock, Joel Spingam, Jim Cross, Lois Woodhull, Handy Hatfield, Constance Williams, Sharmon Donahue, Mildred Seaver, Florence Shaw, Eunice Fisher, W. George Schmid, A. Summers, Robert Hebb, C. Lantis, Dr. Dilys Davies, Diana Grenfell, Loleta Powell, Natalee Suggs and Julia Hardy.

PAUL ADEN

Preface

The title of this book may fail to do justice to the content. True, it is a comprehensive treatment of a most popular genus, but it is more. This book was planned both to help the novice get started, and to serve as a guide and reference for the most practiced gardener as well. The genus is dealt with in the larger context of developing a garden which you can enjoy and be proud of. The approach is practical, based on the years of actual experience accumulated by the authors. Chemical, expensive or labor-intensive recommendations have been consciously avoided.

Thus, the book goes well beyond simply dealing with a single genus, which a brief look at the Table of Contents will confirm.

The co-authors of this book are a quite unique, gathering together of horticultural masters. They live and garden on three different continents. If added up, their gardening experience totals over 300 years. But such a number fails to indicate that the experiences of each is unique. The North American authors do have an advantage, however, as there is little doubt that the hosta hybridizers and growers are well ahead of those in any other country. It will take time for the growers elsewhere to "catch up" as many of them import plants first developed in the United States.

The book has a distinctly international flavor. Some plants which prosper in Japan or England do not do well in North America. This is especially true of the companion plants. The climate in England seems to best compare with that of the Pacific Northwest, while that of Japan relates most closely to the east coast of the United States.

The matter of the nomenclature used in this book deserves a comment. Both Europeans and Japanese tend to use Latinized names for distinctly different forms of hosta, although there is no evidence that many of the plants so named are in fact species. Wherever possible, the nomenclature has been brought up-to-date and in keeping with the current rules, no small task.

The surprise in reading and digesting the thoughts and information from authors of such varied perspective is the wide platform of agreement about gardening and the use of garden plants. Interestingly, all of the authors share many views in common. They have extensive writing experience; extensive gardening experience with the plants about which they write; and are universally highly respected in horticultural circles. And lastly, they love using HOSTAS in solving gardening problems.

Hosta 'Blue Angel', flowering in July.

I

JOHN ELSLEY

Diversity of Hosta

One should hesitate using expressions like "the Perfect Perennial." When all gardening experience is taken into account, such a statement invariably becomes a matter of degree and the personal preferences of the gardener. As an active gardener who has an almost unlimited access to the choicest, hardy perennials available worldwide, it is not difficult for me to say that the *Hosta* genus offers options and advantages to gardeners which very few perennials can equal.

Hostas are basically attractive, foliage plants that prosper in the shade. While they are not evergreen and do not offer a winter display, they do a remarkable job from spring until the frost, the period you spend the most time in your garden. In Japan, they are typically grown as pot plants, used both outdoors and indoors. A year-round display is possible if pots are brought indoors before the cold season sets in. An outdoor plant that can compete as an indoor plant is just one way that hostas can work for the "modern gardener," or someone who is busy with many activities and wants greater mileage from his/her plants.

English and Japanese gardeners have traditionally had a keen appreciation of the value of FOLIAGE in the garden for centuries. Now, entire gardens in which the importance of flowers is subordinated to the use of combinations of long-term displays of the massed colors and textures of foliage plants is becoming a reality in American gardens, particularly during the last decade. Foliage plants are not only easier for the "modern gardener," they offer an extremely long seasonal interest from early spring onwards. Many hosta cultivars, now available, offer an additional bonus, what with new combinations of golds and greens in the late fall. Walking through a temperate garden which includes hostas, one gets the feeling of being cool while the foliage offers a lush, tropical and often architectural look.

It is true that some of the green and gold hostas will prosper in the considerable sun of the "deep south" of the U.S., particularly plants such as *H.* 'Green Wedge', *H.* 'Green Fountain' or *H.* 'Sum and Substance' that have a metallic sheen. Latitude, however, doesn't seem to be as important a factor as the range of temperatures, the altitude and the nearness to bodies of water. However, most hostas perform better with at least some shade in spots where very few other plants can be as impressive.

What is particularly useful about the *Hosta* genus is its sheer diversity. The potential for interest resulting from variation is tremendous, yet at the same time, the opportunities for "clash" in the garden when differing plants are used is minimized. A genus which offers interest through variation at the same time that it offers harmony is worth looking at.

Consider the range in size that the genus offers. *H.* 'Blue Angel' will get to be over 48 in. (1.2 m) high with lush leaves of 14 in. (35 cm) width and over 20 in. (50 cm) in length in an excellent blue color and sumptuous white racemes of flowers in mid-summer. In the same genus, is a very small venusta-type, the deep green of *H.* 'Thumb Nail', no more than

5

Assortment of hosta species and cultivars.

2 in. (5 cm) tall with flower scapes to scale in August.

If you don't want a particular blue or shiny green in a specific spot, the genus offers other blues and greens in various shades, as well as golds and exquisite combinations of colors in the variegated hostas. It is interesting to note that the increasing interest in foliage plants is accompanied by an increasing interest in variegated plants.

Hosta textures offer a particular attraction. I can't think of another genus which offers smooth, glossy, dull, seersuckered and leathery textures. *H. tokudama* 'Aureo-nebulosa', for example offers round, cupped leaves (it traps enough rainwater for a drink) with a fascinating color combination. It also has a puckered texture that plays tricks with low light in the late afternoon.

H. tokudama 'Aureo-nebulosa'

Leaf-shape and habit of mound are offered in a wealth of choices. When you add leaf-shapes in the form of circles, hearts, ovals, lances or straps growing in mounds which may be very formal and symmetrical, ranging through upright or vase-shaped to open and informal, you can appreciate why a good picture is preferable to an adequate word description of hosta plants.

It is generally true that foliage plants are valuable for their foliage—not their flowers. It is relatively rare that a plant has both exquisite flowers and superb foliage. *H. plantaginea* (August Lily) is a special hosta treat with many large (about 5 in. (12½ cm) long and 3 in. (7½ cm) wide), deliciously-fragrant white flowers. While hosta flowers in general may not be outstanding individually, their grouping, setting on the scape, sometimes with interesting scape leaves, at a time when mid-summer flowers are scarce should not be ignored. It is true that some flower scapes are too tall for the mound. Some are too one-sided on the scape and appear unwieldy. Some may be too low in the mound to be properly seen, but improvements have been made with breeding. It is hard to imagine a hosta flower that is an improvement on *H. plantaginea*. Yet, *H.* 'Fragrant Bouquet' offers far more, intensively-fragrant flowers in a large size, with a flat face in front (over 3 in. [7.½ cm]), a more symmetrical distribution on the scape over a very long period of time. Add the magnificent variegated foliage of a bright, apple-green center with a wide, irregular yellow margin which can prosper in considerable sun at the same time that it has very high pest resistance and altogether, everyone must agree, it is a marvelous plant. Also available today are hosta flowers so thickly set to give the appearance of a summer hyacinth. The white, blue, mauve, and purple flowers, often in color combinations, add interest and a "cool" aspect to the summer garden and the summer bouquet. Hosta buds are often a big plus, particularly those with scape leaves which make them look like flowers even before any have opened. *H.* 'Reversed' is a good example. A selection of hostas can be made which will provide flowers from June to the frost. There is no doubt that the vastly improved hosta flowers will create a new set of hosta converts.

Your judgement in selecting plants should depend on the performance of the plants. The word "foolproof" has been vastly overused. Yet, hostas come close to being so with their ease of culture. The very fact that hostas are rarely, if ever, discarded says something about the plants. They are not a "fashion" plant, whose favor will soon be replaced by a newcomer, waiting in the wings. I've never heard of a hosta dying of old-age. In fact, the value of your hostas seem to grow as the plant becomes more beautiful as the years go by, with a minimum of maintenance. It is doubtful that you can find a plant that is completely pest-free, that does not require some staking, spraying, special fertilizing or culture. Hostas come close to the ideal.

Nor need you have a large garden or a staff to benefit from growing hostas, they perform reasonably well even in window boxes of apartments. Smaller gardens offer little opportunity for error in selecting major planting. Hostas offer extra insurance in being able to perform well and "earn their keep." The tremendous surge in hosta use in the last decade is, after all, at least partially accounted for by the greater utilization of hostas by landscape architects, seeking low-maintenance landscapes.

Closeup of flower of *H.* 'Fragrant Bouquet'

H. 'Reversed' showing buds and flowers.

Closeup of foliage of *H. montana* 'Aureo-nebulosa'

The matter of landscape plant selection comes down to WHAT CAN THE PLANT DO FOR YOU? Some gardeners seek a beautiful, individual specimen plant. *H. 'Fascination', H. montana 'Aureo-marginata', H. ventricosa 'Aureo-marginata',* and *H. 'Reversed'* are a few examples of hosta cultivars which will serve such a purpose. Other gardeners seek plants which "mix well" with a great variety of companion plants. Hostas also fit that bill well, particularly in combination with ferns, astilbes, polygonatums and hemerocallis. Beyond these virtues, hostas of the right size and habit make excellent, weedfree groundcovers; superlative edgers to demarcate your beds and walks; huge, lush plants which serve well as background plants; bright foliage to lighten up the dark corners of the garden; superb subjects to add value to evening garden lighting; large specimens to hide eyesores and undesirable objects in the garden, as well as excellent subjects to soften harsh architectural features such as foundations and bare walls. It is no wonder that hostas are discarded so infrequently, they simply do too much for the gardener.

As a full-time plantsman, working to "discover" choice plants, it has been my lot to spend considerable time with the people breeding the hostas of the future. "The present is prologue to the future." Initial observation might lead to concluding that "band wagon" enthusiasm is rampant among those developing new hostas. On closer examination, however, it is obvious that many hybridizers genuinely see vast potential. It is also obvious that the expectations of the gardener are higher than ever before so that only continued, careful breeding will meet this continuously higher target.

Bigger, better-formed, fragrant, artfully-arranged flowers blooming over a long period of time, preceded by attractive buds represent one set of breeder's goals. Appealing foliage with greater sun-tolerance and pest-resistance is another worthy breeder's thrust. The competition is increasing, with the increased discrimination of the public.

Any new hosta introduction must prove itself against a field of very choice, existing hostas before it will be accepted as truly superior. Color quality is no longer enough. Variegation is no longer enough. How the plant performs in a variety of soils and climatic conditions is becoming more important. For example, there is a great interest in developing hostas which will prosper in very warm climates such as Florida or southern California.

One need not possess any great insight to predict that as choicer hostas become more readily available, commercial landscapes will utilize them as never before. They offer too much value not to be used. Public arboreta and private estates are using hostas now in vast quantities. While it is true that growing and propagating facilities now fall far short of meeting the demand, new, very large investments in hosta propagation will eventually "catch up." It has already happened—yesterday's "collector's items" have become today's "standard classics" at prices which the average gardener can afford. For example, not too many years ago, *H. ventricosa* 'Aureo-marginata' sold for $300. This same plant is now being used as a choice groundcover.

H. ventricosa 'Aureo-marginata' used as a groundcover.

H. 'Citation' mound, attractive without flowers.

It is also safe to say that many "lawn-cutters" will be "turned-on" to active gardening as they see more hostas, either in private or public gardens. The return from the plants in terms of satisfaction and pride more than offsets the money and labor outlay involved. Many home gardeners will experiment with growing hostas in pots, as will commercial landscape architects. It is also safe to predict that today's interest in, and knowledge about hostas, will be dwarfed in the next decade.

II

PAUL ADEN

The Cultivation of Hosta

The garden value of hostas can be summed up in three words: foliage, useful and reliable. As trees and shrubs mature, every garden becomes shadier, just as gardeners grow older. The great variety of plants that performed so well while the trees were small are "out of their element" in the shade. In fact, relatively few plants perform well in the shade. The dramatic increase in hosta recognition and use is easy to explain, it is in shady areas that hostas have few peers, so older gardeners find gardening with hostas a pleasanter experience. Hostas have lots of leaf surface from which to evaporate water, as well as plenty of efficient chlorophyll to effectively utilize the small amounts of sunlight that filter through the garden's overhead canopy—the right combination to succeed in cooler temperatures and less light.

When looking for plants which have foliage in various sizes, colors, shapes and textures; which are attractive in the garden from spring until frost; shade the ground so that most weeds can't get started; can happily remain for 30 or more years in one site without any need for division, moving or regular feeding; and become more beautiful as the years go by, the options are rather limited. Driving through very old neighborhoods, while looking for original plantings that have continued to thrive reliably, don't be surprised if the list is rather small, especially if the landscapes are shaded. The search for old plants does have its rewards, not only in discovering the plants that have succeeded with average garden care, have fought off the many afflictions that undo most plants, but in the case of very old hosta clumps, there is an

Old planting of *H. undulata* 'Erronema' at edge of pond with young fish. (Garden of R. J. Meyer)

Mature clump of *H.* 'Blue Mammoth'

added beauty, an added majesty (particularly in larger-size hostas) that only age can confer. In fact, OLDER IS BETTER—in so far as hosta clumps are concerned.

The many color combinations (variegations) in hostas are a big plus, but take some discipline in their use and some understanding of the nature of variegation. We are talking about "living" colors when addressing variegation, colors that are the result of many dynamic processes, involving growth, which result in a range of responses to changes in light, temperature, nutrients and soil conditions, as well as seasonal and rainfall variations. It is readily accepted that young animals look different than mature animals. It takes a bit of experience to realize that the same is true of plants, all plants. Juvenile leaves always look different, but rarely better. Juvenile leaves are not only smaller, but also often have a different shape (i.e., less round) than mature hosta leaves. And there is a very special difference with the colors displayed which creates a difficult problem when photographing plants for use in catalogs. For example, the hosta cultivars *H.* 'Reversed', *H.* 'White Magic' and *H.* 'Wide Brim' have wide, irregular, colorful margins. These marvelous patterns of variegation take some years to fully develop. The shape of the leaf, the range of colors, as well as their arrangement in the leaf-variegation pattern in young plants is often but a hint of the better things to come. Consequently, catalog illustrations, particularly of new introductions, are (or should be) made of mature plants. But this creates a bit of a recognition gap in freshly-planted juvenile plants, a perception which is particularly noticeable with larger hosta cultivars. But this problem corrects itself with passing time, after the plants have matured and acquired their adult variegation pattern.

Juvenile leaves of *H.* 'White Magic'

Mature leaves of *H.* 'White Magic'

Timing and discipline are virtues so intertwined in gardening, it is hard to separate them. But the discipline required in growing choice plants goes a step further. The gardener, bent on increasing the number of newer, choice plants, is tempted to think exclusively in terms of acquiring large numbers of small, juvenile plants, none of which are able to exhibit the basic beauty and character, the real reason for which the plants were acquired to begin with. The perception that the pieces are greater than the whole is with us, but is it true? The gardener, faced with this dilemma, can adopt one of two courses. One option is to simply buy the required number of larger plants, thus realizing immediate landscape effect while they continue to mature gracefully in the desired sites. By analogy, if you like a particular dining chair, and need three more to make a proper setting, the chances are that you will find a way to secure the others and enjoy them as soon as possible. Your outdoor landscape plants are deserving of the same approach. If your landscape plans call for a larger number of plants, buy them, use them and enjoy them.

The other option calls for more patience. Buy a smaller number of plants, but let them grow in one place for three years or so, and then remove divisions. In this way, the landscape plan is not compromised, especially if the small divisions are grown in a special "nursery" area until more attractive for future siting. This exercise of patience will, not surprisingly, result in the same number of plants, but of higher quality than if the gardener had started chopping within the first year of the plant's arrival. Spring of the third year is ideal, as division growth seems to explode at that time.

Section excisions of hosta crowns are almost like removing pieces of a pie. After the noses of the separate divisions have emerged from the ground, then score and cut through the crown and root mass with a sharp, serrated, kitchen knife along the natural dividing lines you have located by removing some of the soil from the crown, and separate the divisions with your fingers, to locate the logical line to make divisions. After the cuts are made, gently lift (with a narrow, sharp shovel or trowel) the excised portions of the plant, complete with roots, disturbing the mother plant as little as possible. A fresh soil mix, set in to fill the void, will remove the evidence of the deed and the missing offset will hardly be noticed. A newly acquired plant is not in its prime. It may have travelled, close-pack fashion, in a truck or in a sealed box waiting at a depot before a trip in the non-pressurized cargo hold of an airplane. Dividing such a small, newly acquired plant, is somewhat similar to surgery. Under the right conditions, all of the smaller patients will survive, especially if given good after-care (such as gentle watering or misting as needed to maintain turgor). But even if the surgery is performed with sharp, clean tools, even if the wound is dipped in a fungicide (such as sulfur, captan or benomyl) and is executed by an experienced master, there will be casualties, as smaller patients are fair game for a host of predators and accidents, seen and unseen.

Time and patience play yet another role in the case of those species or cultivars with large leaf-areas of light yellow, cream or white. These areas contain fewer chloroplasts. If you were to plot a graph of how the rate of growth varies with the number of chloroplasts, you would, not surprisingly, get a straight-line relationship, similar to that in which you find you can achieve greater production by either hiring more workers or working the same number for longer hours. It is no accident that the largest-leafed hostas are one-colored, the green or blue masking the green chloroplasts underneath. Simply put, it takes lots of energy, together with raw materials, and many chloroplasts (workers), to grow large. The chloroplasts (containing green chlorophyll) are the sun's energy-converters which make growth and all other plant processes possible. Differences in amounts of chlorophyll will result in differences in sizes of different cultivars of the same age. Those with little chlorophyll will be predictably smaller, though they may be more interesting in the right setting than the giants. Do not, however, assume that diminutive size equals lack of vigor. For example, *H. venusta* 'Variegated', *H.* 'Squiggles', and *H.* 'Pixie Power' are tiny plants with large white leaf areas, yet they are quite rugged and grow rapidly. In short, such cultivars start their growth with more chloroplasts, the latter becoming fewer as the season progresses

H. 'Pixie Power', few chloroplasts, yet rugged.

(chartreuse areas become whiter). Typically, most small hostas will not only grow rapidly, but also tend to be stoloniferous, which means that they will spread and cover wider areas than you would expect in the years to come. Good examples include: *H.* 'Rock Master', *H.* 'Thumb Nail', and *H.* 'Shining Tot.'

A recent conversation with Alan Bloom, the well-known English plantsman and nurseryman, shifted to his early problems in getting started on land that was relatively cheap, but extremely poor for growing plants. "If I had to do it all over again, I would have started with less, but better quality soil." The quality of the soil (its air spaces, ability to hold nutrients and water, ability to support helpful microorganisms and animals such as earthworms, ability to moderate temperature and the affect of drought) is at least as important as the amount of shade at the site that you pick for a hosta. Two difficult soil types for hostas (as well as almost any other plant) are beach sand (small, round particles, through which water passes rapidly) and clayey soil (that does not allow percolation of water and air). The chances are that if the soil has no animal life, it will be most difficult for plants to prosper without great energy and expense. The man responsible for landscaping Jones Beach, Long Island, recounted that to solve the problems he faced in the early 1930s, salt, wind, and beautiful, but sterile sand, he brought in and plowed under truckloads of peat moss. He then selected plants which could succeed in such circumstances, but which also would build up the soil, over a period of years. These pioneer species were in turn replaced by more desirable plants—definitely not a program for a gardener looking for immediate results. Jones Beach today is considered one of the world's great public parks, and beautifully landscaped.

The Cultivation of Hosta

Average soil, containing about one-third loam, one-third sand (or gravel) and one-third humus to a depth of at least 6 in. (15 cm), at a site that does not bake in the summer sun, suits hostas just fine. Being foliage plants which have large areas through which they transpire (evaporate) water, water-holding ability is the key to soils suitable for hostas. Adding organic materials, such as some packaged, soil-mixes (often including peat moss), compost, leafmold, or well-rotted manure, not only increases water-holding capacity, while retaining air spaces, but also supplies nutrients, the materials—nitrogen, phosphorous and potassium—which are important plant building blocks.

Many gardeners feel compelled to use fertilizer, often for reasons that are not apparent. It is true, that if you plot rate of growth versus the proper amount of fertilizer used, short of poisoning the plant, that you will get a straight-line relationship with most plants. But bigger is not always better, especially with hostas. The surprising thing about artificially feeding hostas is that in many cases, the benefits seem to be minimal, especially if the feeding encourages soft growth that cannot harden off before the onset of winter. This is especially true in the case of potted hostas, left above ground during the winter. In the long-term, building up your soil over a period of time by adding (that means "mixing thoroughly") at least 6 in. (15 cm) in depth organic materials (compost, leafmold, peat moss, well-rotted manure) is preferable. Good cultural practices such as removing spent flowers before they go to seed; neither over nor underwatering (which encourages shallow root growth easily damaged during drought periods); and cultivating, not only to remove weed competition, but also to introduce air into the soil, all add mightily to plant performance.

The big news on weeding in hostas is that such an exercise is minimal, especially when the plants are mature and the leaves of adjacent plants intermesh, leaving little room or light for weeds to get started. The big secret in weeding is timing, which means getting them while they are small, before they rob the soil of nutrients, and when it takes less energy and time on your part to control them. Above all, dispatch the weeds before they go to seed. A long-handled hoe gently moved back and forth, without lifting, and designed to cut close to the clump and get around to the back of the plant, works very well. The design of the Cavex™ hoe, which permits easy access in back of plants, while you are in the front is particularly impressive.

The other news is "not to shoot yourself in the foot" by introducing groundcovers that act like weeds, such as Aegopodium (Goutweed), Honey-suckle, Ivy, Pachysandra, or Oriental Bittersweet. About 2 in. (5 cm) of mulch, applied after the ground has frozen helps to control weeds during the following season. However, too heavy an application, by you or natural leaf-fall, before the soil has frozen, may encourage mice to take up residence in the area, and mice, when pressed, will eat nearby hosta rhizomes during the winter, especially when heavy mulching allows the mice to dig.

Foliage plants, such as hostas, evaporate (transpire) large amounts of water, acting like "living air-conditioners," but only if the soil has the water to begin with. If for no other reason, all plants need a certain amount of water to maintain their turgor (another way of saying "to avoid wilting"), so watering practices, especially during drought periods, does require some care. Guide lines on watering hostas:

1. Water slowly, so as not to compact soil, or encourage soil erosion, or beat surface indumentum off hosta surface (particularly blue hostas).

2. Water deeply, at least 1 in. (2.6 cm) of water (as measured in an open container), or enough to penetrate the soil at least 6 in. (15 cm) deep.

3. Water during the forenoon, before it gets too hot, so as to give plants a chance to dry somewhat before nightfall (when slugs are most active).

Hosta foliage transpires (evaporates) large amounts of water. *H.* 'Mikado' shown.

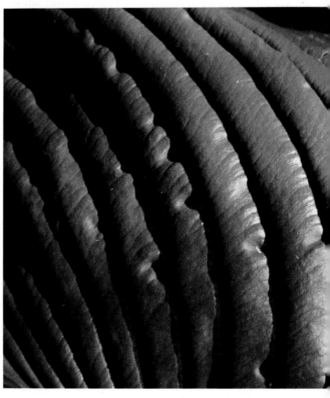

Hostas grown in the shade have fewer, but larger leaves.

If your plants are not performing well, fertilizer may help, particularly if the soil contains little organic material or intrinsic nutrients. Well-balanced fertilizers, containing nitrogen (in nitrates, ammonium radical); phosphorus (in phosphates or phosphoric acid); potassium (in potash or wood ash); and trace elements are recommended. It should be understood that different genera have different nutrient requirements, making a one-patent-formula for the type of fertilizer and dosage for all plants impossible. This difference in nutrient needs helps to explain the variation in natural habitat and plant preferences. The special advantage of the natural habitat is that the debris from previous season's growth decomposes and can be recycled by bacteria for use by the plant in a new season. It should be noted that plants cannot distinguish between organic or chemical fertilizers, but the danger of overdosage is much greater when much more soluble in water chemical fertilizers are used. If a plant is only slightly short of nutrients, a large application of fertilizer will not help. On the contrary, excessive amounts may promote the destruction of cells (particularly in the roots), well illustrated by Roman armies, when they added insult to injury after they sacked and pillaged an enemy (victim) by pouring salt over the croplands as they left. Excess fertilizer works just as did the Roman salt, in causing critical amounts of water to leave, rather than enter the roots, resulting in either death or wilting, or at best producing flaccid, succulent growth which is more easily damaged by pests, diseases, drought, or cold, as well as encouraging soil microorganisms that cause rot. Again, the virtues, discipline and moderation, dictate using only what is necessary.

First try a slow-feed fertilizer (Osmocote 14-14-14 or other slow-release fertilizer) at about one-half of the recommended dosage. Apply in the spring preferably and mix into the soil after growth has started. Fertilizer applied before the plant is ready or able to use it, may benefit many microorganisms, but may kill the plant. A weak foliar (Peter's Professional 20-20-20) fed once every two weeks can work wonders, particularly during periods of active growth. Start using about 1/10th of the recommended dosage. Avoid foliar feeding during the hottest part of the day.

In general, the more heat your hostas experience, the more moisture and air-retentive your soil should be. This is especially true for young plants that are not established. The greater the amount of moisture in the soil (short of eliminating all of the air spaces), the larger the leaves will be. Shade conditions tend to induce fewer, but larger leaves as well as a reduction in flowers and seed production. The largest leaves wait until the clump is established before they show up.

The Cultivation of Hosta

Up to the point of causing the foliage to shrivel, more light tends to produce more hosta plant divisions, greater seed production, and more, but smaller, leaves. Less light produces fewer divisions, fewer seeds and larger leaves. In Holland, hostas are grown in full sun for maximum propagation (caution—lots of water is available in that land of canals which reaches roots by capillary action). This kind of siting may be great for the nurseryman, but hardly makes sense for the home gardener. Please understand that nursery catalogs advising where to site a plant are suggestions, a starting point. The final arbiter on siting is the plant. If the plant prospers, you were very wise in your siting. If the plant is struggling with no obvious cultural cause, the reasons can vary from it being a weak plant to a subject worthy of a committee study. But while you are waiting for the committee's report, experiment with a new site, if only with a division from the plant. In fact, plan to do some experimental moving, at least of some cultivars, before the ideal site is found, one in which the foliage texture, size, color and variegation are at their best. Hosta clumps are relatively easy to move, particularly in the spring. And it should be noted that moving them, at almost any time, in the search for improved landscape effect, is a satisfying, creative undertaking when you are trying to master the principles of landscape design. With care, hostas can be moved at any time the ground is workable, and the soil is sufficiently moist to maintain the root-soil mass during moving (typically, the day after watering). The trick is to avoid breaking too many root hairs, the plant organs necessary for nutrient and water uptake.

When the soil is hard and sun-baked, brown margins on hosta foliage may develop, particularly in the yellow or white areas of the leaves (where less chlorophyll is present), particularly during long periods of summer drought. Anything you can do to make the soil more moisture-retentive (i.e., incorporating compost, leafmold or peat moss*), more air-retentive (also helped by *) and more nutrient-retentive (also helped by *) not only makes life easier for hostas but also a lot easier for you.

Whenever a significant gap between the rate of water evaporation (transpiration) from the leaves and water absorption from the soil by the root hairs develops, you will have an unhappy plant. Avoid watering during the hot part of the day (i.e., 2 PM). Early morning is ideal as it gives the plants a chance to dry somewhat before the onset of evening and potential slug invasion. Slow-feed watering through porous hoses is preferable to overhead watering. Cold water from a sprinkler, hitting hot leaves puts the leaf cell structure to a difficult test as the cell walls

have to shrink in too little time. This is something like diving into ice water fresh from a sauna, only more disastrous for the plant. Plants with large leaf surfaces relative to their mass (certainly includes hostas), suffer considerable cell wall rupturing if subjected to cold water. Tests have shown that mature hosta plants often get through the summer better with minimal watering. This is especially true of hosta foliage with a wax, luster or indumentum surface-finish.

Mature foliage with lustrous finish requires minimal summer watering. *H.* 'Sum and Substance' shown.

Closeup of indumentum of blue hosta foliage in the spring. (A. Viette)

The indumentum of blue hostas, such as *H.* 'Blue Angel', *H.* 'Blue Moon', *H.* 'Love Pat', and *H.* 'True Blue' absorbs most of the colors in the white light spectrum, reflecting only blue light. While some blue genera do well under desert conditions (*Yucca* for example), and even look attractive, the blue surface substance of hosta foliage can be damaged by long-term exposure to excess heat. The surface seems to almost melt off. "Blues" are at their best in cool, shady spots, and if possible, close to bodies of water. The water not only moderates the ambient temperature, but also supplies continuing, higher humidity. These meliorating circumstances enable the surface cells to reorganize themselves, restoring the "blue." The waxy bloom on the leaves act like hair-like filaments that attract the water molecules (hygroscopic) contained in cooler, moister air masses, resulting in a curling and aligning of the filaments that are responsible for reflecting blue light. Siting near bodies of water, in greater shade, in more moisture-retentive soil, as well as in a more northerly exposure, or at higher elevations all produce a longer-lasting "blue." In general, avoid rubbing blue foliage or allowing high-pressure water sprays to hit it over long periods.

Gold hostas, such as *H.* 'Gold Edger', *H.* 'Little Aurora', *H.* 'Midas Touch', *H.* 'Shade Master', *H.* 'Sum and Substance', *H.* 'Sun Power' and *H.* 'Zounds' reflect light and heat well. While they tend to develop their best color in strong light, they achieve a remarkably bright color in the shade. In fact, they noticeably brighten a dark, unnoticed area of the garden. The 'golds', and whites, such as *H.* 'Celebration', *H.* 'White Colossus', or *H.* 'White Magic' are particularly pleasing when planted in combination with "blues," a good example of the whole being greater than the sum of the parts.

Gold foliage develops best color with more sun. *H.* 'Midas Touch' shown.

Sprite', *H.* 'Shining Tot', *H.* 'Thumb Nail' and *H. venusta* 'Variegated'.

EDGER hostas (*H.* 'Blue Wedgwood', *H.* 'Gaiety', *H.* 'Ginko Craig', *H.* 'Golden Tiara', *H. tardiflora* and *H.* 'Vanilla Cream') are low, and neat with vigorous horizontal growth. Adjacent plants mesh, leaving no room or light for weeds. By overhanging a lawn edge, the time spent in edging is reduced. Surround trees or shrubs in mid-lawn with hosta-edging plants. Mowing, then, is not ony easier, it is safer. Edgers should have less visual impact than foreground plants.

The overhanging of a lawn edge by hosta foliage reduces the time spent in lawn edging. *H.* 'Ginko Craig' shown.

The use of hostas depends mainly upon their size. Bearing in mind that size varies somewhat with culture and age, hostas are SMALL—8 in. (20 cm) or less; EDGER—12 in. (30 cm) or less; GROUNDCOVER—18 in. (45 cm) or less; BACKGROUND—24 in. (60 cm) or more; and SPECIMEN—any size. Hostas grown in pots are always smaller and more juvenile in their leaf character.

SMALL hostas are much more rugged than you might expect. They not only succeed, but are quite attractive in rocky places containing little or poor soil. They work well in difficult places, such as among tree roots or on a slope. Some suggestions for these sites are: *H.* 'Blue Moon', *H.* 'Chartreuse Wiggles', *H.* 'Little Aurora', *H.* 'Pixie Power', *H.* 'Rock Master', *H.* 'Sea

GROUNDCOVER hostas can be bigger, even somewhat stoloniferous, which makes them especially useful in binding soil on slopes and reducing erosion. Good examples include *H. gracillima* 'Variegated', *H.* 'Ground Master', *H.* 'Hadspen Blue', *H.* 'Shade Fanfare', and *H. ventricosa* 'Aureomarginata'. Hostas do an outstanding job in areas difficult to weed or maintain. They act like a "living mulch"—not ony cutting down on the need to weed, but also the need for extra watering. At the same time, they keep the soil cool for spring-flowering bulbs and wildflowers. They tidy up unsightly areas. In broad expanses, hosta groundcovers present a dramatic, yet restful panorama.

Hostas control soil erosion on a slope. *H.* 'Ground Master' shown.

Hostas can tidy up unsightly areas. *H.* 'Ground Master' shown.

The larger, BACKGROUND hostas (*H.* 'Big Mama', *H.* 'Blue Umbrellas', *H.* 'Fringe Benefit', *H.* 'Green Wedge', or *H. montana* 'Aureo-marginata') overlap hostas suitable as groundcovers. In terms of clothing the bare earth, they are hard to beat. They tend to be lush with an exotic, tropical aspect which tends to give a sense of privacy to a patio or place where people may relax. While tall hosta foliage will not completely block out prying eyes, it does give a sense of a significant barrier to demark your own "turf." Their intrinsic interest lies in their color, texture, architecture and sheer size.

SPECIMEN hostas (*H.* 'Citation', *H.* 'Fascination', *H.* 'Reversed', *H.* 'Fragrant Bouquet', or *H.* 'Wide Brim') can be of any size. They deserve to be placed close to the viewer, as they demand at least a second look. The mound form, color pattern, leaf texture, fragrance or shape and size of the flower or a combination of these make the intrinsic detail elements more enjoyable—and worthy of a closer look. Specimen hostas refute the myth, repeated by too many nurserymen and landscapers, that a plant's interest begins and ends with its flower. Specimen hostas are performers for many months, attractive, even in nurseries. Their mounds sit on the ground like giant, beautiful flowers.

An example of a specimen hosta. *H.* 'Wide Brim' shown.

III

DR. SAMUEL B. JONES, JR.

Hosta As Viewed By A Botanist

Although hostas have been cultivated in China and Japan for centuries, they did not become known to western botanists and horticulturists until about 1790 when the first two species arrived in Europe from China (Grenfell, 1981). These two Chinese species are the familiar *H. plantaginea* and *H. ventricosa*, both widely grown in many gardens today. They were the only species of *Hosta* in Europe until some 40 years later when von Siebold, a Dutch nurseryman who lived in Japan for several years, brought back a number from Japan. For the next 35 years or so until his death in 1866, von Siebold distributed hostas widely over western Europe. From England and continental Europe, hostas travelled to the New World to be used as ornamentals. In the late 19th Century, American travelers to Japan, such as Thomas Hogg, began to send collections of living hostas to the United States, a practice that continues today.

NOMENCLATURE

The nomenclatural history of *Hosta* began in 1780 when the Swedish botanist Peter Thunberg, a former student of Linnaeus, applied the generic name *Aletris* to one of the two Chinese species of *Hosta* (Bailey, 1930). Four years later, Thunberg apparently realized that *Hosta* should not be grouped with the other members of the genus *Aletris*, and so placed the plants in the genus *Hemerocallis*, the familiar Daylilies so widely grown in our gardens. For many years, hostas remained in *Hemerocallis*, but plant taxonomists recognized that Hostas were distinct from daylilies and should not be associated together in the same genus. In 1812, the Austrian botanist, Leopold Trattinick, removed them from the daylilies and published the name *Hosta* to honor the Austrian botanist, Nicholas Host (Hylander, 1954).

Unfortunately, Baron von Jacquin, Director of the Botanical Garden at Vienna had already applied the Name *Hosta* to a genus in the Verbena family. However, Jacquin's use of *Hosta* itself was invalid because Linnaeus had previously named the same group in the Verbena family. Under the rules of nomenclature, Linnaeus' name had "priority", which means the oldest name is normally the one that must be used. Further, under the rules of botanical nomenclature, once a generic name has been used, even if incorrectly, it cannot be applied to a different group of plants. Thus, Trattinick's *Hosta* became an illegitimate name.

Five years later, in 1817, Kurt Sprengel corrected the situation by publishing the name *Funkia* for our plants—a name used throughout the 19th Century, and one that still appears, albeit incorrectly, in some catalogs, and at a few garden centers. It would seem that our nomenclatural journey would end here, but in 1905, the International Botanical Congress, the governing body for plant names, voted to conserve the name *Hosta*. In this way, Trattinick's name, *Hosta*, was made legal by a vote of the Congress some 83 years after Trattinick first proposed it. Today, the names of the species of *Hosta* are regulated by the International Code of Botanical Nomenclature and the plants of garden origin, known as cultivars are dealt with by the rules found in the International Code of Nomenclature for Cultivated Plants. The University of Minnesota Landscape Arboretum, jointly with the American Hosta Society serves as the official international registrar for the cultivars of *Hosta*.

As generally recognized by botanists today, *Hosta* includes perhaps 20 or more species with two from China and the remainder found in Korea and Japan (Fujita, 1976a). The genus is not well understood by botanists and the number of species has varied greatly depending upon the species concepts used by the various authors. Also adding to the nomenclatural confusion is the uncertain status of a number of cultivars introduced by von Siebold, but named as if they were species found in the wild (Henson, 1985). Taxonomically, the genus is subdivided into two subgenera: *Niobe* and *Bryocles*. Subgenus *Niobe* has ony one species, *H. plantaginea*; with the remainder of the species included in subgenus *Bryocles*.

Newcomers to hostas are often bewildered by hosta nomenclature and by the confusing array of names for species and cultivars. We have seen how some of the confusion began even with the naming of the genus itself and its introduction into the western world. Further, from the beginning there was a lack of detailed published descriptions and pressed and dried herbarium specimens needed for thorough botanical documentation (Hylander, 1954). Until relatively recently, the genus has been incompletely known to western botanists and attempts by westerners to unravel the classification have not included all of the Oriental species. *Hosta* has been examined by many notable botanists, including L. H. Bailey (1930), W. T. Stern (1931), and Nils Hylander (1954), and their efforts have improved our knowledge of the group. The Japanese botanist, Fumio Maekawa spent a lifetime attempting to classify the species of *Hosta*, publishing his work in 1940 with minor revisions over the next 40 years. Maekawa's species appear to be narrowly defined and inflated in number. Recently, his work has largely been superceded in the botanical world by that of Noboru Fujita, a Japanese ecologist, who published his classification of *Hosta* in 1976. Unfortunately, Fujita's treatment does not appear to have been widely accepted by horticulturists.

While botanists were struggling with the naming and classification of the wild species, amateur and professional horticulturists had been making crosses, growing thousands of seedlings, selecting unusual variations and in the process, naming hundreds of cultivars. Through the work of the American Hosta Society and the University of Minnesota Landscape Arboretum, much progress has been made in stabilizing the names of the cultivars. The latter is by no means an easy task with the tremendous range in leaf shape, color, size, and variegation patterns typical of the genus. Also, the plants vary according to the growing conditions at the site, as well as the age of the individual clumps which can significantly modify the appearance of the plants.

WHAT IS A *HOSTA*?

Botanists are often asked the question, "What makes a plant a *Hosta*?" That question appears simple enough, but it is not easily answered. In non-technical terms, *Hosta* are described as clump-forming, rhizomatous, long-lived perennial herbs, having many spirally arranged leaves radiating out from the base of the crown (Dahlgren, et al., 1985). The leaves may be long and narrow, or egg-shaped to almost heart-shaped in outline.

As Professor Dahlgren and his associates pointed out, in some *Hosta*, the section between the expanded blade and the basal sheath is termed a peudopetiole because while it appears to be a petiole, it is actually blade tissue. Hidden below the ground are compact crowns of stem tissue which botanists call rhizomes. In some species and cultivars, the rhizomes may be somewhat elongate and spreading. Both buds and roots grow from the rhizomes. At the proper season, the buds ("eyes") produce leaves and flower stalks. The fleshy roots form a dense mass radiating from the rhizomatous crown and are seemingly capable of retaining water. Although absent from the stem and leaves, the roots contain xylem vessels, large water-conducting cells unique to flowering plants.

Moving on to the reproductive structures of *Hosta*, the flowering stalks or scapes are conspicuous and surpass in height the surrounding foliage. The flower cluster itself has one main axis which carries the individual flowers on short stalks or pedicels. This type of flower cluster is termed a raceme. The flowers are not evenly spaced on the raceme. The raceme appears somewhat one-sided in many plants. Modified leaves, termed bracts are found along the scape and at the base of each pedicel. The bracts vary considerably in size and shape among the species and cultivars of *Hosta*.

The flowers are bisexual and range from pure white to deep blue, to various shades of lilac and purple, often with white stripes. The six conspicuous

Some examples of typical hosta flowers. *H. montana* 'Aureo-marginata' shown at left. *H. fortunei* forms shown in foreground.

segments of the flower (sepals and petals) are similar in appearance and for this reason are termed tepals. The tepals form a bell-shaped or trumpet-shaped structure and are variously united at their bases. The six stamens or male part of the flower each consist of a pollen producing anther and a supporting stalk called the filament. The filaments are attached either to the lower inside of the tepals, or just below the seed producing ovary.

The central portion of the flower or the female part is the pistil with the ovary at the base, and a slender stalk or style, terminated by a 3-lobed stigma. In the process of pollination, the pollen grains land on the stigma where they germinate and produce a pollen tube. The pollen tube grows through the pistillate tissue carrying the sperm to the young ovule. Following fertilization, the ovule develops into a seed. Botanists describe the pistil as being compound since it is composed of three parts or carpels which are fused together. The ovary has three chambers called locules, one derived from each carpel. The numerous ovules are attached in two rows in each locule to the center of the ovary. When

mature, the ripened ovary becomes dry and splits from the tip into three parts. Botanists classify this type of ripened ovary or fruit as a capsule. The seeds are black to brownish, flat with a thin wing extending above the plump embryo or immature plant. When the ripened capsule opens, the seeds tend to hang to the central part of the capsule, revealing their point of attachment to the ovary itself.

CHROMOSOME SIZE AND NUMBER

Much of the genetic code needed to control the growth and development of plants is carried by the chromosomes of plants located in the nuclei of the cells. In certain tissues of plants undergoing active cell division, such as root tips, it is possible to observe with a light microscope the size, shape, and number of chromosomes of plants. The array of chromosomes of a cell, when visualized by the appropriate techniques, is termed the karyotype. By the 1930s, botanists realized that the karyotypes of the plants could be used in developing classifications, or groupings of related plants, and began to compare the karyotypes of many plant genera. For example, *Yucca*, which had been previously classified in the Lily family and *Agave* assigned to the Amaryllis family were found to have similar karyotypes with 10 large chromosomes and 50 small chromosomes. Taxonomists used this and other evidence to establish the Agave family where both *Yucca* and *Agave* may be found today.

Shortly afterwards, the Japanese cytologists Akemine (1935), and Matsuura and Suto (1935) discovered that *Hosta* has a similar karyotype with 12 large chromosomes and 48 smaller ones. Immediately, some botanists proposed that *Hosta* should be placed in the Agavaceae rather than in its usual home in the Liliaceae. Today, the karyotype evidence seems less important because other genera referred to the Agavaceae on the basis of their *Agave/Yucca* type of growth form do not have similar karyotypes. In fact, now that more plants have been studied, the combination of a few large and more numerous small chromosomes is not uncommon in the Lily line of monocots, but it does not correlate well enough with other features to be of assistance in classification (Cronquist, 1981).

Since the 1930s, botanists have studied the chromosomes of *Hosta* and found that most of the species have 60 chromosomes in their somatic cells and 30 chromosomes in their reproductive gametes. This is of importance to breeders of hostas in that plants with the same chromosome number are more likely to form successful hybrids than plants with different chromosome numbers. However, it is interesting to know that there are exceptions to the chromosome number. One of the species from China, *H. ventricosa* has plants with the standard 60 chromosomes, but some plants have double that number. The individuals with 120 chromosomes are called tetraploids. Another species, *H. clausa*, is called a triploid because it has 90 chromosomes.

A species, *H. ventricosa* has tetraploid forms. *H. ventricosa* shown. (Dr. S. B. Jones, Jr.)

BREEDING SYSTEM

Since the 19th century, it has been recognized that hybrids may be made between the majority of the species and cultivars of *Hosta* either by random insect pollinations or through controlled pollinations by breeders. It has also been observed that many hostas set seed regularly even when grown in isolation. Thus hostas appear to be normally self-fertile, so breeders must remove the anthers of the female parent when making crosses. To the gardener, this means that seedlings of open pollinated plants are unlikely to come true due to cross-pollination by insects flying among the hostas, especially if more than one species or cultivar of *Hosta* is being grown nearby.

Horticulturists have noted that certain garden hybrids or cultivars of *H. undulata* and *H. lancifolia*, as well as some of the cultivars derived from the *H. fortunei* line, usually fail to set seed and hence are female sterile. It has also been observed that these same plants produce high percentages of infertile pollen grains. When reduction division, or meiosis, was examined in the cells that give rise to the pollen grains, it became apparent that abnormalities in the hybrid chromosome complement of the cells of these plants were responsible for the male and female infertility (Kanazawa and Akemine, 1975). These findings explain why certain cultivars are sterile or nearly sterile.

A species, *H. undulata* flowers fail to set seed and shed spent flowers quickly. *H. undulata* shown.

One of the most phenomenal breeding situations occurs in *H. ventricosa* (Hylander, 1954). First noted in 1810 by the amazingly perceptive English botanist, Robert Brown, the seed of *H. ventricosa* develop vegetatively from maternal tissue in the ovule. The process is asexual and seed are produced without the union of egg and sperm. Botanists refer to the process as agamospermy, a phenomenon found in a number of unrelated plant families and one that is often associated with polyploidy. As noted earlier, *H. ventricosa* is a polyploid. The significance of this is that the seedlings of *H. ventricosa* will all be identical to the mother plant and thus "come true" from seed.

Horticulturists are constantly searching for unusual forms or modifications in plants such as variegated leaves. From a somewhat different approach, botanists have attempted to explain how the variegation is inherited. In 1929, the Japanese cytologist, Yasui, made a series of experimental crosses between variegated and green forms of *Hosta*. She found that the normal rules of Mendelian inheritance did not apply, that variegated offspring could only be obtained when the female parent was variegated. Yasui concluded that variegation was inherited by some unknown means from the maternal parent. Using the light microscope, Yasui also observed variation in the plastids of the variegated plants. About 50 years later, Vaughn and associates published a series of papers utilizing electron microscopy and improved knowledge of modern cell biology, confirming that variegation in *Hosta* is inherited maternally, and that the trait is controlled by non-nuclear genes carried in the plastids. This technical information is invaluable to the breeder desiring to develop variegated plants. In other words, if variegated offspring are desired, a variegated plant should be used as the female parent.

ECOLOGICAL STUDIES

Noboru Fujita (1976b, 1978a, b) recently examined the habitat preferences and water requirements of the Japanese hostas. He found that the species which commonly occur in a diversity of soil moisture conditions, such as *H. sieboldiana,* can adapt their water economies to a wide variety of habitats and should be regarded as unspecialized. On the other hand, *H. kikutii* and *H. longipes,* which are restricted to rocky outcrops, have a low transpiration rate and are drought-resistant. Finally, *H. longissima,* which is confined to wet places, exhibits low drought-tolerance. Fujita also reported correlations between the species' natural habitat and their flooding-tolerance. For example, *H. sieboldii* and *H. longissima,*

which occur on wet soils, show high tolerance to flooding. Basic ecological information such as this is very useful in a modern breeding program to provide cultivars adapted to a wide variety of ecological habitats.

H. sieboldii forms show high tolerance to flooding. *H. sieboldii* 'Haku-Chu-Han' shown.

RELATIONSHIPS OF HOSTAS TO OTHER PLANTS

Traditionally, the genus *Hosta* has been placed in the family Liliaceae, and further classified in the tribe Hemerocallideae. Genera included in the tribe were: *Hemerocallis* (Daylilies), *Hosta, Leucocrinum,* and *Hesperocallis,* the latter two genera having only one species each and occurring in the southwestern United States.

Recent protein comparisons suggest affinities between *Hosta* and both the Agavaceae and *Camassia* of the Hyacinthaceae. In 1985, in the most recent treatment of the families of the monocots, Professor Dahlgren and his fellow researchers (1985) placed *Hosta* in the family Funkiaceae along with *Leucocrinum* and *Hesperocallis*. The Daylilies are placed in their own family, the Hemerocallidaceae. Neither *Leucocrinum* nor *Hesperocallis* are particularly similar to *Hosta*, or to each other, but various features suggest relationships. Dahlgren clearly points out that the position of the Funkiaceae is uncertain. It should be noted that their treatment is characterized by rather narrowly defined families. It should also be pointed out that the lily line of monocots poses a difficult challenge to plant taxonomists who are attempting to develop a meaningful biological classification showing true affinities among these plants. Work is in progress at the University of Georgia comparing the flavonoid pigments and the soluble enzymes of species of *Hosta* and related genera which will hopefully resolve some of the questions regarding phylogenetic relationships of *Hosta* both at the specific and generic levels.

APPLICATION OF BIOTECHNOLOGY TO HOSTA

In recent years, many exciting discoveries with potential practical applications have been made in the biological sciences. Words such as genetic engineering, genes, DNA, tissue culture, etc., have become commonplace and their practical application is known as biotechnology. Tissue culture (micropropagation) technology is being used with hostas. For example, hostas are usually propagated by crown division. Introduction of a new cultivar can take several years as relatively few buds or "eyes" are produced annually on the rhizomes. However, the introduction of new cultivars can be greatly speeded up by taking some of the tissue from young developing flower clusters, sterilizing it and placing the tissue on suitable nutrient, sterile medium. By proper manipulation of the plant tissue with nutrients, hormones and light, hundreds of plants can be cultured from a single, young flower cluster. This technique does not work with all species or cultivars. It does require rigid quality control by highly trained technicians working with specialized laboratory equipment. The consistency of plants produced this way is typically higher as fewer cells are involved as a starting point. This has been especially true with many variegated clones. The tremendous increase in hosta use and popularity can be accounted for, in no small way, by this availability of some very choice, new cultivars at affordable prices, propagated by using tissue culture techniques.

At the United States Department of Agriculture Research Center at Beltsville, Maryland, work is in progress in an attempt at intergeneric crosses between *Hosta* and Daylilies. Chromosomes are being transferred between the genera. The USDA researchers hope to develop a shade-tolerant Daylily, or a *Hosta* with unusual colored, Daylily-type flowers, just to mention a few possibilities. If successful, there may be a number of potential applications leading to the production of new and at least unique cultivars of *Hosta*, or whatever the plants will be called. At the Botany Department of Miami University in Ohio, attempts to overcome the sterility problems in crossing certain hostas have been successful in using protoplasts (plant cell contents without the cell wall) produced from callus tissue grown in nutrient culture (Miller and Wilson, 1981). The protoplasts are then fused and hybrid plantlets regenerated from the fused protoplasts. This procedure has potential in developing new cultivars that were never before possible. In the next 20 to 30 years, other new developments from plant molecular biology will be applied to *Hosta*.

While some recent cultivars are snail and slug resistant, while some recent cultivars can be grown in full sun, while some recent cultivars have large, well-formed, fragrant flowers, this may become a matter of course in all of the new hostas. The possibilities are exciting and unlimited.

REFERENCES

Akemine, T. 1935. Chromosome studies on *Hosta*. The Chromosome Numbers in Various Species of *Hosta*. *J. Fac. Sci. Hokkaido Univ.*, Ser. 5, Bot. 5:25–32.

Bailey, L. H. 1930. *Hosta*, the Plantain Lilies. *Gentes Herbarium*. 2:117–142.

Cooke, J. F. 1968. *The Chromatography and Cytology of Some Cultivated Taxa of the Genus Hosta*. PhD. Dissertation. Ohio State University. Columbus.

Cronquist, A. 1981. *An Integrated System of Classification of the Flowering Plants*. Columbia Univ. Press. New York.

Dahlgren, R. M. T., H. T. Clifford, and P. F. Yoe. 1985. *The Families of Monocotyledons*. Springer-Verlag. Berlin.

Fujita, N. 1976a. The genus *Hosta* (Liliaceae) in Japan. *Acta Phytotax. Geobot.*, 27:66–96.

_____. 1976b. Habitat and Water Economy of Japanese *Hosta*. *Jap. J. Ecol.*, 26:71–81.

_____. 1978a. Flooding Tolerance of Japanese Hosta in Relation to Habitat Preference. *Mem. Fac. Sci. Kyoto Univ.*, Ser. Biol. 7:45–57.

_____. 1978b. Reproductive Capacity and Leaf Development of Japanese *Hosta* as Viewed from

Ecology and Evolution. *Mem. Fac. Sci. Kyoto Univ.,* Ser. Biol 7:59–86.

Grenfell, D. 1981. A Survey of the Genus *Hosta* and its Availability in Commerce. *The Plantsman,* 3:20–44.

Henson, K. J. W. 1963. Identification of the *Hostas* ("Funkias") Introduced and Cultivated by von Siebold. *Meded. Landbouwhogeschool,* Wageningen., 63:1–22.

————. 1985. A Study of the Taxonomy of Cultivated *Hostas. The Plantsman.,* 7:1–35.

Hylander, N. 1954. The Genus *Hosta* in Swedish Gardens. *Acti Horti Bergiana.,* 16:331–420.

Kanazawa, H. and T. Akemine. 1975. High Frequent Occurrence of Chromosome Breakage in PMC's of *Hosta un dulata. La Kromosomo.,* 100:3108–3117.

Maekawa, F. 1940. The Genus *Hosta. J. Fac. Agri. Tokyo Univ.,* Sec. 3 (Bot.). 5:317–425.

Matsuura, H. and T. Suto. 1935. Contributions to the Idiogram Study in Phanerogamous Plants. *I. J. Fac. Sci. Hokkaido Univ.,* Ser. 5, Bot. 5:33–75.

Miller, P. D. and K. G. Wilson. 1981. Protoplast Fusion and Organ Culture in the Genus *Hosta. Envir. Exp. Bot.,* 21:431–432.

Stearn, W. T. 1931. Hostas or Funkias. *Gard. Chronicle.,* 2:27, #47–49, #88–89, #110.

Vaughn, K. C. and K. G. Wilson. 1980. Genetics and Ultrastructure of a Dotted Leaf Pattern in *Hosta. J. Hered.,* 71:121–123.

IV

PAUL ADEN

Hostas with Latinized Names

Species are plants found growing naturally in the wild, and which perpetuate themselves in the wild (typically from seed), are the basic building blocks used by botanists in grouping plants. While there continues to be much dispute as to the number of *Hosta* species, their grouping (classification), as well as in which species individual plants should be placed, there is no doubt that they are primarily native to Japan, with a lesser number from China and Korea. The typical, botanically innocent gardener should be able to recognize written references to a species by its Latinized name (some Greek is occasionally used), in which the genus name is given first, followed by the species name, followed by the cultivar name i.e., *Hosta tokudama* 'Aureo-nebulosa'. Please note that the genus is italicized or underlined and is written or printed entirely in lower case and starts with a capital letter, that the species is italicized or underlined in lower case letters, and the cultivar name is enclosed in single quotes, but in Roman type. Linnaeus had hoped that this system, devised by him, would end the unbelievable confusion, which surrounded the naming of plants in the eighteenth Century, but he failed completely to reckon with human nature. While there are probably no more than 20 distinct *Hosta* types that meet the standards required to be recognized as a species, well over 100 *Hosta* plants are sold under Latinized names, at least 80 of which are garden varieties, chance seedlings, not to be found in the wild. So, if you pollinate, allow the seed to form and cast the seed of a choice plant

like *Hosta tokudama* 'Aureo-nebulosa', do not hold your breath waiting for a lot of little editions of the same.

No one scientific publication names and describes all of the *Hosta* species, or even those with incorrect Latinized names. Any attempt to do so is well beyond the scope of this book, and would only add more confusion than light to the nomenclature problem. Many consider that the work, published in 1940 by the Japanese botanist, Dr. Fumio Maekawa (1908–1984), who spent five years studying hostas in the wild before publishing his dissertation on hostas, as one of the best. After a memorable day examining plants and discussing the *Hosta* "species problem" with Dr. Maekawa, no easy answer emerged. After a day of examining and discussing *Hosta* with Dr. Noboru Fujita, who has spent close to 20 years studying *Hosta* in the wild, and who has published a monumental work on the subject including not only morphological, but also the ecological information, again yielded no easy answers. And just to keep the taxonomic pot boiling, a new species was recently discovered on a remote island off the coast of North Korea. Much of the difficulty is that many species are polymorphic in the wild, that is, they tend to mutate, compounded by the fact that wild plants are located at sites difficult to access. The problem of sorting out the *Hosta* species has involved some of the best international, botanic minds including the Swedish botanist, Nils Hylander, the Engiishman, William Stearn, and the American, Liberty Hyde Bailey,

Dr. Fumio Maekawa (1908–1984) published one of the widely accepted classification schemes for *Hosta* in 1940.

among others.

Nearly all of the hostas having Latinized names have resided in my garden. As I start this chapter, without the training or desire to be a taxonomist, a tune called "Fools rush in . . ." can be heard in the background. However, I will attempt to call out the unique "identifiers" of each, and indicate how hostas with Latinized names may be used. Look for illustrations of some of the better forms.

The meaning of some of the information in the descriptions is as follows:

Number in ( ) = # required/sq. yd. (Multiply by 1.2 for # required/sq. meter). For EDGERS: number in ( ) = # required/running yd. (Multiply by 1.1 for # required/running meter).

SMALL: 8 in. (20 cm) or less in height, suitable for the rock garden.

EDGER: 12 in. (30 cm) or less in height, vigorous horizontal growth; not stoloniferous.

GROUNDCOVER: 18 in. (45 cm) or less in height, frequently stoloniferous; to reduce maintenance and bind soil.

BACKGROUND: Lush, architectural, 24 in. (60 cm) or taller in height, can be used to increase privacy.

SPECIMEN: Any size, sited close to the viewer to enjoy detail, texture, color pattern, buds, flower or fragrance.

H. albomarginata See *H. sieboldii*

H. capitata Korea, Shikoku; Groundcover; dark green with a sheen, heart-shaped leaves, 3 in. (7½ cm) wide, 5 in. (12½ cm) long and 7–8 pairs of veins, which have beautifully "piecrust" leaf margins; flowers are gathered together in a tight ball-shaped purple bud with large bracts, from which up to 20 congested purple flowers emerge in summer; flat mound 18 in. (45 cm) in diameter and about 10 in. (25 cm) high; scape is nicely purple dotted, and rises to a height of 18 in. (45 cm), with definite ridges along its length; (4); shade to ¾ sun.

H. cathyana See *H. gracillima* 'Variegated'.

H. chibai Groundcover; 5–8 branches on the main flower scape at least; lilac-colored flowers in September; quite floriferous; dome-shaped mound 14 in. (35 cm) high and 18 in. (45 cm) in diameter; elm-green leaves are oblong and heart-shaped, 7–8 in. (17½–20 cm) long and 4 in. (10 cm) wide; (4); shade to ¾ sun.

*H. clausa** Korea; Groundcover; well-suited for controlling soil erosion; violet buds in summer, but flowers never open; quite stoloniferous; mound is 8 in. (20 cm) high and 8 in. (20 cm) in diameter; lance-shaped, dark green, sharp-pointed, shiny leaves are about 1 in. (2½ cm) wide and 5 in. (12½ cm) long with 4–5 pairs of veins; carried on a short petiole; 15 in. (37½ cm) scape with about 20 buds is smooth, round and purple-dotted near the base; horizontal buds have reddish bract; (20); shade to ¾ sun.

H. crispula Groundcover; white, irregular, wavy margin on the dull, very dark-green leaf; dome-shaped flat mound to 28 in. (70 cm) in diameter and 16 in. (40 cm) high; oblong, egg-shaped leaves with long, tapering tips that droop and often twist under, are 4 in. (10 cm) wide and up to 8 in. (20 cm) long, 7–8 pairs of veins, held on long, arching petioles; 36 in. (90 cm) scape is green and topped with 30–35 closely spaced flowers of a pale lavender color in late June; protect from strong wind; (2); shade to ½ sun.

H. decorata Groundcover; leaf tips rounded; flat mound 18 in. (45 cm) in diameter and 10 in. (25 cm) high; somewhat stoloniferous; leaves have regular, slightly wavy, silvery-white margin, 3 in. (7½ cm) wide, 4 in. (10 cm) long, rounded tips, 5–6 pairs of veins, matte green; 24 in. (60 cm) high

H. clausa (Dr. S. B. Jones, Jr.)

H. crispula (Dr. L. E. Cannon)

H. decorata (Dr. S. B. Jones, Jr.)

H. fluctuans 'Variegated'. Note upright form of mound.

scape, topped with a dozen small, urn-shaped, dark lilac flowers in summer; (4); shade to ½ sun.

H. elata Background; large, wavy-leafed, dark-green hosta, of upright growth, up to 30 in. (75 cm) high, 30 in. (75 cm) diameter; heart-shaped leaves 8 in. (20 cm) wide and 12 in. (30 cm) long, with 9–11 pairs of veins, on long erect petioles; at the petiole, the leaf is pinched together; tip is very long and pointed. The 60 in. (150 cm) scape bears 20–30 funnel-shaped, pale purple flowers with yellow anthers on a long raceme in summer; (1); shade to ¾ sun.

H. fluctuans 'Variegated'* (*H. montana* 'Sagae') Background, Specimen; twisted leaves emerge early in spring with wide, irregular wavy margins of bright yellow, frosted gray-green base; upright, vase-shaped mound 24 in. (60 cm) high and 36 in. (90 cm) diameter; heart-shaped leaves truncated and pinched at petiole; tip elongated and sharp, 10 in. (25 cm) wide, 12 in. (30 cm) long, 9–10 pairs of veins; 48 in. (120 cm) scape with many purple-suffused, whitish flowers in summer; plain green form grown as vegetable in Hokkaido; (1); shade to ¾ sun.

H. fortunei types. Groundcover; dome-shaped mounds, about 14 in. (35 cm) high, 24 in. (60 cm) wide; leaves are 4–7 in. (10–17½ cm) wide and 9–12 in. (22½–30 cm) long with 9–11 pairs of veins; emerge late in the spring; 36–48 in. (90–120 cm) scapes with pale purple, funnel-shaped flowers in early summer; (2); shade to ¾ sun.

H. fortunei 'Albo-picta' Bright yellow leaf with a crisp, dark, green margin. The yellow slowly changes to light green and finally becomes a uniform, dark green.

H. fortunei 'Albo-marginata' Wide, white margin that remains until frost.

H. fortunei 'Aureo-marginata' Yellow-gold margin on a dark, spinach-green leaf; (2); shade to ¾ sun.

H. fortunei 'Gloriosa'* Thin white margin on lance-shaped, furrowed leaves.

H. fortunei 'Hyacinthina' Greenish gray frosty looking bloom. It later turns to a uniform gray-green; (2); shade to ¾ sun.

*H. gracillima** Small; shiny-green, wavy, lance-shaped leaves, 4 in. (10 cm) long and less than 1 in. (2½ cm) wide, with 3–4 pairs of veins; mound 5 in. (12½ cm) high and 8 in. (20 cm) in diameter; leaf blunt at base, tip twisted sometimes; scape with 8–10 funnel-shaped, recurved, purple-suffused flowers in September; (25); sun to ½ sun.

H. gracillima 'Variegated' (possibly *H. cathyana*, old name for *H. lancifolia* 'Variegated') Small; also groundcover, to control soil erosion; green base with neat yellow to cream margin; rounded tip, stoloniferous; lavender flowers in summer; (10); shade to ¾ sun.

H. helonioides 'Albo-picta' Groundcover; creamy-yellowish margin with bright green base; mound 10 in. (25 cm) high and 24 in. (60 cm) diameter (when mature); leaves very elongated with a slightly rounded tip; 1 in. (2½ cm) wide, 7 in. (17½ cm) long with 3–4 veins; 24 in. (60 cm) high scape, somewhat purple-dotted at base with up to 20 purple-striped flowers, held horizontally in late summer; (4); shade to ¾ sun.

H. fortunei 'Gloriosa'

H. fortunei 'Hyacinthina' (Dr. S. B. Jones, Jr.)

H. helonioides 'Albo-picta' (A. Viette)

H. gracillima 'Variegated'

Hostas with Latinized Names

H. hypoleuca

H. kikutii (Dr. S. B. Jones, Jr.)

H. lancifolia (Dr. S. B. Jones, Jr.)

H. longissima (Dr. S. B. Jones, Jr.)

*H. hypoleuca** (Urajiro) Groundcover; powdery-white coating on the back of the leaves that remains all season, a "white-back" hosta. In nature, this hosta hangs on rock cliffs, with clinging roots; gray-green leaves, 12 in. (30 cm) wide, 15 in. (37½ cm) long, up to 8 pairs of veins; mounds 12 in. (30 cm) high, about 22 in. (55 cm) wide; scape about 24 in. (60 cm) with almost white, lightly purple-suffused flowers in early summer; (3); shade to full sun.

H. kikutii Varies widely in wild (polymorphic), beak-like bracts surround the flower buds; low transpiration rate, drought-resistant; slightly wavy, glossy-green leaves, 3 in. (7½ cm) wide, 9 in. (22½ cm) long, 8–10 veins on short petioles; leaves lance-shaped with heart-shaped base, tapering tip drooping at end; mound 12 in. (30 cm) high, 16 in. (40 cm) diameter; scape is up to 30 in. (75 cm) high, rigid, light green and has several large, leaf-like bracts; around 20 near white flower racemes in summer; (8); shade to ¾ sun.

H. kiyosumienses Groundcover; elliptical-ovate leaves 6 in. (15 cm) long 2 in. (5 cm) wide, 5–6 veins; yellow-green above; shiny on underside; mound 6 in. (15 cm) high, 10 in. (25 cm) wide; 15 in. (37½ cm) scape with few erect-spreading, white flowers; anthers pale dirty purple; (12); shade to ¾ sun.

H. lancifolia Small; somewhat stoloniferous; glossy, oblong, dark-green leaves grow to about 2 in. (5 cm) wide and 6 in. (15 cm) long, 4–5 pairs of veins and an elongated sharp tip; clumps about 12 in. (30 cm) high and 18 in. (45 cm) wide; flower scape 22 in. (55 cm) high, purple-dotted at the base; many trumpet-shaped, purple-suffused flowers with bluish purple anthers in summer; (6); shade to ½ sun.

*H. longipes** Groundcover; varied group in wild often on shaded rocky outcrops, often near stream beds; drought-resistant; purple-dotting on the petioles and scape, sometimes also spotted on the leaf base; slightly wavy, dark-green leaves are 3 in. (7½ cm) wide and 6 in. (15 cm) long, with 7–8 pairs of veins; elliptical outline with a pinched, heart-shaped base; 12 in. (30 cm) mound, about 16 in. (40 cm) in diameter; scapes 12 in. high with profuse, bell-shaped flowers of light purple suffused white (sometimes blue) flowers, held horizontally on long pedicels; (6); shade to ¾ sun.

H. longissima Small; bogs, flood-tolerant, but not drought-tolerant; strap-shaped, glossy-green leaves, ¾ in. (2 cm) wide, 7 in. (17½ cm) long, 3 pairs of veins, blunt tip; appear to rise directly from the crown in an arching fashion; mound 6 in. (15 cm) high, 10 in. (25 cm) in diameter; many erect scapes, reaching 20 in. (50 cm) high, with few dilated, funnel-shaped, pale violet flowers, with dark, colored veins in the corolla, in late summer; (15); shade to ½ sun.

H. montana

H. montana* Background; varies in the wild, leaves typically emerge quite early in spring; dark, matte-green, shaped like an elongated heart, with an incised base, 11 in. (27½ cm) wide and to 20 in. (50 cm) long with 14–17 pairs of deeply impressed veins held stiffly erect on strong petioles in an arching fashion, with the tips drooping; mound 30 in. (75 cm) high and to 48 in. (120 cm) in diameter; scape 50 in. (125 cm) high, straight and erect with 25 near-white, trumpet-shaped flowers bearing bluish purple anthers in early summer; (1); shade to ¾ sun.

H. montana 'Aureo-marginata'* Background; varie-gated form which emerges early in spring; leaves huge, slightly-wavy, glossy-green base with wide, irregular yellow margins, elongated heart-shaped, 10 in. (25 cm) wide, 14 in. (35 cm) long, 13–14 im-pressed leaves with tapering, drooping point; mound 26 in. (65 cm) high, 40 in. (100 cm) diam-eter; scape 40 in. (100 cm) high with many funnel-shaped, densely-arranged, pale lavender flowers in early summer; (1); shade to ¾ sun.

H. montana 'Sagae' See *H. fluctuans*

H. nakaiana* Edger; heart-shaped, wavy, dark-green leaves, 2 in. (5 cm) long, 1 in. (2½ cm) wide, 5–6 veins; long petioles, purple-dotted near base; mound 6 in. (15 cm) high, 12 in. (30 cm) wide; many scapes to 18 in. (45 cm), with a purple-dotted base; has many, tightly bunched, pale purple flowers in summer; (9); shade to ½ sun.

H. nigrescens* Background; slightly-wavy, oval, gray-green, leathery leaves, 7 in. (17½ cm) wide, 11 in. (27½ cm) long, 12 pairs of veins; mound 20 in. (50 cm) high, and 24 in. (60 cm) diameter; 60+ in. (150 cm) scapes with many near white, funnel-shaped flowers in midsummer; (3); shade to ¾ sun.

H. nigrescens 'Elatior'* Varies from the species in that it has shiny, green, larger leaves, taller scape, up to 9 ft. (2¾ m) high; larger flowers, up to 3 in. (7½ cm) long and is more sun-proof; (1); shade to full sun.

H. nigrescens in foreground contrasted with *H. nigrescens* 'Elatior' in the background.

H. opipara Groundcover; egg-shaped, slightly wavy leaves with glossy green base and yellow margin; 7 in. (17½ cm) long, 5 in. (12½ cm) wide, 9 pairs of veins, margin yellow extends into petiole wings; flat mound, 24 in. (60 cm) wide, 14 in. (35 cm) high; 32 in. (80 cm) scape with lilac, funnel-shaped flowers in summer; (3); shade to ¾ sun.

H. plantaginea* (August Lily) Background, Specimen; Chinese species; large, waxy, fragrant, white flowers; leaves almost round, heart-shaped, 7 in. (17½ cm) wide and 10 in. (15 cm) long with 9 pairs of impressed veins, bright glossy, yellowish green; mound 24 in. (60 cm) high and 35 in. (90 cm) wide; 30 in. (75 cm) scapes with trumpet-shaped flowers up to 3 in. (7½ cm) wide at the lobes and 5 in. (12½ cm) long in August; (1); shade to ½ sun.

H. pulchella* Small; varies in wild; stoloniferous; glossy, green leaves ½ in. (1 cm) wide 3 in. (7½ cm) long; mound 1½ in. (4 cm) high, 6 in. (15 cm) wide; 4–6 in. (10–15 cm) scape leans somewhat with lavender flowers in July; (36); shade to ¾ sun.

H. pycnophylla* Specimen; extreme "pie-crusting" of margins with white underside; leaves 8 in. (20 cm) long 4 in. (10 cm) wide; mound about 12 in. (30 cm) high 18 in. (45 cm) wide; blue, trumpet-shaped flowers in August; (4); shade to ¾ sun.

H. pulchella

H. plantaginea (Dr. S. B. Jones, Jr.)

H. sieboldiana with Bleeding Heart. (A. Viette)

H. rectifolia Groundcover; varies in wild; gray-green leaves are winged and glaucous throughout length, are erect, 6–10 in. (15–25 cm) long 2–2½ in. (5–6 cm) wide, 6–9 veins on each side, the blade oblong acute, petiole has the same length as the leaf; mound 15 in. (37½ cm) high, 22 in. (55 cm) wide; scape is round, fairly stout, 23–30 in. (57½–75 cm) high with purple buds followed by many large, violet, erect at first, flowers with short green bracts with purple stripes into the middle (persisting after flowering), in summer; (4); shade to ¾ sun.

H. rhodeifolia Groundcover; leaves with yellow margins, 10–12 in. (25–30 cm) long, 3 in. (7½ cm) wide, of lance-like or oblong shape, shiny green base with 5–6 veins; 30 in. (75 cm) scape with lavender, funnel-shaped flowers in summer; (9); shade to ½ sun.

H. rupifraga* Groundcover; varies in wild; subtropical growing on rough, rocky mountain sides; leaves are green, leathery, shiny, wavy, somewhat twisted with sharp tips, 3–6 in. (7½–15 cm) long, 2–3 in. (5–7½ cm) wide, 6–8 impressed veins, pale veins are elevated; petiole is rigid and thick; green, but splashed and fused with purple, 1–3 in. (2½–7½ cm) high, grooved with margins rolled inward; mound 10 in. (25 cm) high, 15 in. (37½ cm) wide; rhizome is short and thick; short scapes with dense racemes of lavender, violet or purple flowers that bloom in fall; leathery bracts with purple margins; (6); shade to full sun.

H. shaishu jima Small, green wavy leaves ½ in. (1 cm) wide, 4 in. (10 cm) long; mound 3 in. (7½ cm) high, 6 in. (15 cm) wide; scape 10 in. (25 cm) with purplish flowers in mid-summer; (36); shade to ¾ sun.

H. sieboldiana Background; varies widely in nature; adapts well to very moist or relatively dry conditions; leaves are round, blue-green, seersuckered, with bloom that fades in warm weather; 12 in. (30 cm) width, 14 in. (35 cm) long, 12–14 pairs of veins deeply impressed; mound (in 5 years) to 30 in. (75 cm) high and 52 in. (130 cm) wide; scape is barely tall enough to reach the topmost leaves, with thickly-clustered white (center of lobe only diluted with purple tinge) flowers placed on one side in early summer; (1); shade to ½ sun.

H. sieboldii (*H. albomarginata*) types: Small; found on wet soils, high flood-tolerance; at first glance, looks like *H. lancifolia*, but has yellow anthers instead of bluish-purple; wavy leaves are lance-shaped and small, a little over 1 in. (2½ cm) wide and 4–5 in. (10–12½ cm) long, with 3–4 pairs of veins, color above is matte, dark-green, below shiny, lighter green; mound 12 in. (30 cm.) high, 12 in. (30 cm.) wide, scape 20 in. (50 cm), with 2–3 sterile, leafy bracts along the stem, slightly bell-shaped, whitish flowers in August with deeply colored purple veins; (9); shade to ½ sun.

H. sieboldii (Dr. S. B. Jones, Jr.)

H. sieboldii 'Kabitan'

Hostas with Latinized Names

H. undulata 'Univittata'

H. ventricosa in flower.

H. undulata 'Variegata' (Dr. S. B. Jones, Jr.)

H. ventricosa 'Aureo-marginata'

H. undulata 'Erromena' Groundcover; leaves medium green, erect, ovate, bluntly contracted, tapering gradually, 7–9 in. (17½–22½ cm) long, 5–5½ in. (12½–13½ cm) wide, shiny, 10 veins; petiole 18 in. (45 cm) long, jade-green, channeled with base dotted purple; mound 20 in (50 cm) high, 26 in. (65 cm) wide; scape 32 in. (80 cm) high, round and with 2 or 3 bracts; bracts long ovate, base acutely clasping and green; (3); shade to ½ sun.

H. undulata 'Univittata' Leaves rather plain with clear white center stripe that varies from ¾–1½ in. (2–4 cm) wide, ovate, turns down near tips; leaves turn down to make a rounded mound, 18 in. (45 cm) high, 24 in. (60 cm) wide; may sport to all green variety, H. undulata 'Erromena'; (3); shade to ½ sun.

H. undulata 'Undulata' See H. undulata 'Variegata'.

H. undulata 'Variegata' (also called H. undulata 'Undulata') Small; leaves with white splashes and streaks through center area, green margin, quite wavy, 5 in. (12½ cm) long, 3 in. (7½ cm) wide, oval-heart-shaped, with a spiral-twisted, elongated tip, 8–10 pairs of veins; petiole edged with white on outside, red dots at base; mound 10 in. (25 cm) high and the same wide, rounded, mounds vary as leaf arrangement in mound is random; scape 32–40 in. (80–100

cm) tall, often arches, sterile leaf-like bracts, small, pale purple, funnel-shaped flowers on one side of scape; (16); shade to ½ sun.

H. ventricosa Background; leaves slightly wavy, shiny underside, heart-shaped with tapering pointed tip, dark-green leaves, 5–7 in. (12½–17½ cm) long, 3½–5 in. (8–12½ cm) wide with 8–9 veins; mound 24 in. (60 cm) high, 36 in. (90 cm) wide; many scapes to 36 in. (90 cm), round, rigid with suffused red at base, a single bract in the middle; 20–30 bell-shaped, violet flowers with bluish stripes in summer; (1); shade to ½ sun.

H. ventricosa 'Aureo-maculata' Groundcover; variegated (spring only), irregular yellowish-green center with a dark green margin, center coloration darkens with the onset of warmer weather, finally turns into a uniform dark green; (2); shade to ½ sun.

H. ventricosa 'Aureo-marginata'* Groundcover; leaves heart-shaped with a unique twist, broad, irregular margin of yellow that turns to white (lasts until frost) dark green base, 6 in. (15 cm) wide, 7 in. (17½ cm) long; mound 18 in. (45 cm) high, 24 in. (60 cm) wide; many mauve flowers in midsummer; (4); shade to ¾ sun.

H. venusta (Dr. S. B. Jones, Jr.)

H. venusta* Small; Korean species; slightly wavy, green leaves are heart-shaped and pinched at the squared-off base; 1 in. (2½ cm) long and 1 in. (2½ cm) wide, 3–4 pairs of thin veins; mound no more than 4 in. (10 cm) high and 8 in. (20 cm) wide, stoloniferous; petioles and scape has a distinct parallel grooving; 10 in. (25 cm) scape with 4–8 funnel-shaped, (that expand) violet flowers with darker veins in the lobes in early summer; (25); shade to ½ sun.

H. venusta 'Variegated'* Small; cream center with two-tone green margins; center chartreuse in early spring; mound 6–8 in. (15–20 cm) high, 6 in. (15 cm) wide, stoloniferous; (36); shade to ¾ sun.

In 1968, when the American Hosta Society was organized, the names of known cultivars were listed. *Hosta Registration* was discussed in the following article:

We are registering the names of hosta cultivars (i.e. horticultural varieties) to avoid the confusion which would arise through the use of duplicate names for different hostas. At the moment, there is probably less than a hundred that have been named. In the future, there will likely be several hundred and even thousands. Most everyone realizes the confusion that we now face with the species and botanical varieties. Certainly we must avoid further complications.

Anyone that has in the past named any hostas is also requested to register these names. This list will be published annually in the Hosta Bulletin. If available, a short description of the plant and who introduced it will be included. This will help other hosta enthusiasts to keep informed on what is available.

A pleas to all those who propagate, hybridize and to others connected with the distribution of hostas: Use officially registered names. In the past some have been guilty of dubbing species with cultivar names in order to increase the selling price of the plant. This should cease. Another thing we must avoid is naming unworthy seedlings. Be certain the plant merits naming.[1]

By writing to the Minnesota Landscape Arboretum, International Hosta Registrar, 3675 Arboretum Dr., P. O. Box 39, Chanhassen, MN 55317, registration forms for hostas can be obtained. Detailed descriptions and color slides showing both the flowers and foliage are required, along with a $2 fee for each cultivar registered.

Today, at least 600 hosta cultivars have been formally registered. The use of proper names for cultivars, as well as species is complicated by some outlets offering seedling hybrids for true species and the confusion of "sports" in both cultivars and species sold under the name of the parent plant. The fact that so few outlets offer an adequate display of mature plants or good pictures and descriptions in catalogs makes the reputation of the outlet a most important element in obtaining true-to-name plants.

The title of this chapter, *Hosta with Latinized Names,* does not indicate that the plants described are true species or necessarily among the best choices in hybridizing or solving landscape problems. Many of the plants described are expensive and rare. The better ones will be propagated and distributed. Many of the "discard" hybrid seedlings in my own hybridizing program, for example, are better than most of the plants listed in terms of flowers, pest resistance, sun tolerance, vigor and solving special garden problems. Prices between the more common plants described in this chapter and the newer cultivars has become competitive in recent years. Hybridizers, like research scientists starting out, are advised to "climb on the shoulders" of the best workers that preceded them. A * has been placed after the names of those plants that have special qualities that do make them suitable for either hybridizing or landscape work. The chapter dealing with "Recommendations for the Landscape" does include many hostas included in this chapter.

---

[1]"Hosta Registration" of the *American Hosta Society Bulletin #1*

V

YOSHIMICHI HIROSE

Hosta Enjoyment and Cultivation in Japan

H. montana, self-sown in the wild.

It may be said that the Japanese islands are a "Treasure Island" for the collectors and growers of wild hostas. Japan's total land area is 378,000 km^2, about the size of the state of Montana. Of this, 250,000 km^2 is forest. By no coincidence, this is a figure very close to the area that is mountainous, 268,000 km^2, and cannot be used for agriculture or habitation. Fortunately, while wild hostas continue to thrive in areas "unfit" for human habitation, they have been moved down to where the people are—around homes, in the landscapes around shrines and temples. Hosta leaves have been used to clothe Buddha statues as well as to construct platforms (looking like rafts) for the statues to sit on. The heavy shade in the mountains forbids normal vegetable crops, but farmers in rugged, shady areas of mountainous Hokkaido grow, sell, and cook some hostas (mainly young leaves and petioles) as a vegetable crop. The typical Japanese home is set on a very small plot, so there is an especial interest in the small hosta species, tremendous interest in the variegated forms and typically a wide use of pot-culture in growing and displaying hostas. Hosta exhibits are common throughout Japan.

Plant hunting in the wild for new forms is widespread in Japan. It is not unusual for families to spend their weekends climbing in the rugged mountains looking for interesting and different forms. As over 80% of Japan is mountainous and sparsely settled, there is much area to explore. Until quite recently, the main interest was confined to discovering new forms

Spacious home garden, by Japanese standards, of Dr. Y. Tsukamoto in Kyoto, Japan. Note the use of small hostas.

which occurred naturally. The idea of artificially "bred cultivars" is relatively new among hosta fanciers in Japan. It seems that the Japanese people have simply taken hostas for granted.

All that is rapidly changing. The recent discovery of some spectacular variegated hostas in the wild has created a tremendous interest and perhaps new opportunities. Many of these new variegated forms, some rather bizarre, others rather puny, have been found in areas where waste nuclear fuel had been dumped. While it is not certain whether these new variegated hostas are natural seedlings, normal sports or sports induced by radiation, this outcome is unexpected as finding variegated hostas growing in the wild is a rare occurrence. Bearing in mind that the variegation of these new hosta discoveries require at least four years to confirm their stability, it is worth mentioning a few which certainly warrant further watching. At present, the prices of these rare hostas, if even offered for sale, are frequently in the range of thousands of dollars:

1. *H. longissima* 'Aureo-marginata'
2. *H. longipes* 'Hakuho'
3. *H. longipes* 'Okutama-nishiki'
4. *H. montana* 'Choukou-nishiki'
5. *H. montana* 'Hatsusimo'
6. *H. montana* 'Kinkaku'
7. *H. pulchella* 'Aureo-marginata'
8. *H. rectifolia* 'Aureo-marginata'
9. *H. tardiva* 'Aureo-marginata'
10. *H. venusta* 'Variegated'

Mass plantings of non-variegated hostas are rarely seen in masses in Japan. The Japanese appreciation of variegated foliage plants, with hostas among the favorites, whether in public and private gardens, is largely focused on single plants. Retail garden centers and flower shops in Japan typically sell hostas, usually the more common kinds, as single plants in attractive glazed or painted pots, sometimes in combination with grasses or other plants to make a small arrangement. The species and cultivars most widely available:

1. *H. undulata* (Suji-giboshi)
2. *H. tokudama* 'Aureo-marginata' (Tokudama-kifukurin)
3. *H. tokudama* 'Aureo-nebulosa' (Ko'akebono-tokudama)
4. *H. decorata* (Otafuku-giboshi)
5. *H. rhodeifolia* (Omoto-giboshi)
6. *H. albomarginata* (Koba-giboshi)
7. *H. crispula* (Sazanami-giboshi)
8. *H. lancifolia* 'Kabitan' (Kapitan)
9. *H. lancifolia* 'Haku-Chu-Han' (Shiro-kapitan)
10. *H. gracillima* 'Aureo-marginata' (Mimeiwa-giboshi-kifukurin)
11. *H.* 'Kisuji-giboshi'

H. montana 'Choukou-nishiki'

H. venusta 'Variegated', potted in typical Japanese style. (Y. Hirose, Japan)

At this point, I would venture that the reader has made the connection between the word "giboshi" and hosta. But what the reader cannot know is of the prices of these ordinary, potted hostas, typically very small clumps, which are on the high end of the nursery-price scale, even by United States standards—a clump of *H. tokudama* 'Aureo-nebulosa' can easily cost over $70, for example.

In North America and Europe, an increasing number of the people are growing the numerous forms of hosta, usually as in-ground, landscape plants. Garden centers and mail-order outlets report no problem in selling hostas, especially if mature clumps are included in the display. Their main problem is replenishing sales stock. Hostas used to tend to be much larger than those seen in Japan. Massed plantings of hostas in public and private estate gardens, mainly as groundcover and background plants, have accelerated the awareness of hostas. In Japan, hostas have traditionally been regarded as nice, "native garden plants", typically enjoyed as single specimens and not used to solve landscape problems. The steady growth of the economy and better living conditions, especially in the last few decades, has rekindled the Japanese enjoyment of gardening. The typical Japanese-style or western-style house and garden is small by western standards. Yet, hostas are considered as one of the most suitable garden landscape plants.

H. fluctuans 'Variegated' used as a potted plant at home entrance in Tokyo, Japan.

Currently there is great interest in making rock-garden settings, which is not difficult in rocky Japan. While the emphasis remains on small, variegated hostas, in older, larger gardens the medium and larger sizes are also used, often in association with other popular plants such as arum, arisaema, acorus, calanthe, fern, astilbe, asarum, hakonechloa, polygonatum and disporum, typically in artistic arrangements in shady environments. But just as the Japanese buy hosta as a pot plant, they typically use them as pot plants in the garden, but above ground, or on a veranda, or near the entry or inside the home.

Growing hosta in pots requires better attention to watering, as the soil dries out faster than in the garden. In general, water slowly (so as not to compact soil) and abundantly so that excess water comes out of the bottom of the pot. Water only when the top surface feels dry to the touch, or a flick of the finger on the side of the pot produces a hollow sound. The soil should retain moisture, and food, but also air. An equal mix of coarse sand, loam and peat moss (or leaf mold) is quite satisfactory. A small amount of slow release, organic fertilizer can be mixed into the top surface after the plant has started to grow in the pot, generally in the spring. Hostas like a slightly acid pH (about 6) soil, but are remarkably tolerant in this regard. Glazed or nonporous pots (plastic), retain water better, but there is danger of overwatering, particularly if stones or crock chips to a depth of about 1 in. (2.5 cm) are not placed over the bottom openings. Pots sunk in the ground need extra drainage holes. While it is true that potted hostas with good root systems survive under slightly dry conditions for long periods of time, a summertime drought can kill the plants in pots, particularly if the pots are above ground and exposed to sunlight.

When a hosta begins to outgrow its pot, either trim the roots or pot up to the next size. Early spring, just as new growth is about to start, is the ideal time. It should be noted that potting, over a period of years, has a "bonsai" effect on hosta plants. The leaves are not only smaller, they are less round and more spear-shaped. The variegation pattern also differs. Many color gradations do not develop, which is typical of a juvenile plant. Pot culture is particularly desirable for growing a wide variety of forms. Further, there is considerable satisfaction in having your favorite garden plants thriving indoors during the winter when the garden is drab. It is easy to move from one room to another as occasion demands—moving fragrant hostas or those possessing delightful variegation or buds about the house is especially tempting. Potted hostas in bathrooms are especially welcome.

Be cautioned that bringing outdoor hosta pots indoors can present problems. The indoor environment, lacking the natural predators which control harmful insects, permit mites, insects (such as aphids) and even nematodes to thrive, presenting problems that are not important out-of-doors. Spray your plants carefully before bringing them indoors, particularly on leaf-undersides and notches where insect eggs may be deposited. A very weak, soapy solution—1 drop of dish detergent to about 1 quart (liter) of water is effective. Timing of transfer indoors is important—best before the temperature falls below 45°F (8°C). If temperatures have gone below this level, allow the plant to go dormant in a cool

room for about a month before moving indoors to light, warmth and moisture. Check the plant carefully durng the first month for signs of insect or mite problems, while populations are low, particularly in hot and dry locations. Another forceful spray with weak soapy water, particularly on the underside of leaves, is a good ounce of prevention.

Collectors or connoisseurs of anything in the world continually search for the unique, the new and the rare. So it is with hostas. In Japan, hosta collectors are like ardent lovers in search of new forms, especially different patterns of variegation. Many of the choicest plants, few in number, and typically in private collections, are only to be shared with a few select friends. These rare forms are often considered priceless. Even the offer of a Rolls Royce may be insufficient to convince a serious Japanese collector to part with a small division of his choicest plant. The serious collector may be coaxed to "trade," but only for a plant perceived to be of equal merit. The more commercial (example: nurseryman) the negotiator for a rare plant is, the more likely that the price will be extremely high or that a trade will be impossible to arrange. Two presented in this class are: (1) *H. venusta* 'Albo-medio-picta', a tiny plant with a white center and green margin, (2) *H.* 'Reiho', a very small, somewhat upright form with a chartreuse to cream base and an irregular two-tone green margin; red petioles.

There are but three means to obtain these rare hostas in Japan:

1. Discovery by chance in the wild or in the growing areas of nurseries. The probability of success is vanishingly small, despite the fact that unique forms have been discovered in this way. But it is worth noting that a lot of Japanese are looking.

2. Acquisition from owners by purchase or exchange. Success often depends on "knowing" the owner, on having a good character and reputation and being able and willing to pay a very high price.

3. Controlled hybridization, including the use of radiation or chemical mutagen techniques, typically done on a large, commercial scale. The use of radiation or chemical mutagens requires special training to be done safely. It stands to reason that a radiation or chemical mutagen dosage sufficient to cause a genetic change in plants may also be sufficient to cause genetic change in humans. It is instructive to note that most genetic changes are negative in character. The probability of developing a unique form with stable variegation and which does not lose normal plant vigor is extremely low. A slightly greater degree of success has been achieved employing intense micro-propagation procedures. In this case, many

clonal generations are produced using tissue culture technology, with the tiny plants grown on nutrient agar medium containing growth hormones and under aseptic conditions. Even the relatively few cases of success using micropropagation must be grown on for a period of time to insure that the plants have stable variegation and retain a sufficient measure of vigor.

It is most important to make a rigid evaluation of seedlings before they are selected for introduction. The presence of variegation in a seedling is no longer the main criteria for introducing a hosta cultivar. Equally important objectives include:

1. Flower fragrance.
2. Better golden or blue foliage.
3. Better or unique form, size or color of the flower.
4. Use as an edible vegetable, which makes hostas one of the few vegetables which will grow well in the cloudy, shaded conditions of mountainous Japan.
5. Strong vigor and resistance to pests.
6. Capable of being grown and marketed at an affordable price.

When I talk of my hope of creating new variegated hostas, it is the 'Streata' (streaked in the center) type that I particularly have in mind. 'Streata' variegation has been well developed in the U.S.A., but the existing cultivars in Japan are yellow forms of white 'Marginata' or 'Medio-picta' types. A particular problem with trying to create new 'Streata' types is that they typically revert to 'Marginata' or 'Medio-picta' types in time. Some plantsmen contend that a good result is realized when reversion takes place, but the hope for a truly stable 'Streata' type is, of course, the most desirable, as it is so rare.

My experience in hybridizing hostas has made me aware of a number of factors of which I was not aware when I started. Many species and cultivars seem to be sterile. This is especially disappointing as sterility seems to be characteristic of the most beautiful forms, almost as it you are being told that the "ultimate" has been reached. Further experimentation will be required before viable seed from desired crosses is developed.

1. Make crosses in a greenhouse to gain optimal temperature control. It may be that the ambient summer temperature in Japan, when most crossing is done, is too high.

2. Study the chromosomal makeup of desirable parents. It could be that some potential parents are polyploid or have other unique chromosomal characteristics.

3. Examine pollen under the microscope at different times of day to determine the best conditions for gathering and using pollen.

4. Experiment with different time-frames for both gathering and storing seed before planting.

5. Vary the temperature and conditions under which seed is stored. It could be that some seeds have a very short "shelf-life".

6. Experiment with excising the embryo from the seed while it is still alive.

In closing, I think it useful to note a seeming contradiction: that while the hosta genus could be described as including the "perfect perennial," at least under conditions of shade, it is also the genus to which a great deal of recent exploration and search for new forms is being devoted.

Marinated hosta petioles served as a vegetable. (M. Kamo, Japan)

H. 'Flamboyant', example of a "Streata" type of variegation.

VI

MABEL-MARIA HERWEG

Flower Arranging with Hostas

While not new to either gardens or to flower arranging, as hostas were introduced into Europe in the eighteenth century, and into North America in the nineteenth, that handful of original Hosta species imported from Japan, China and Korea were only infrequently used in flower arranging. Though useful, the early, primarily green-leafed, hostas had little impact. The case is entirely different today, thanks to the richness of form and color now available. Whether species or modern hybrids, hostas are especially useful in helping the arranger convey her (his) floral message for all to behold and enjoy.

Any genus characterized by varied leaves and flower forms and which can add line, mass, form, size, scale, texture and color is, at the least, useful in flower arrangement. But, given the spectacular leaf and flower forms and colors of the modern hostas, they can hardly be recommended too forcefully as a superior source of arranging material. For example, hosta flowers such as *H. plantaginea* (common name = August Lily), a species from China, are white, large and fragrant and can be substituted for Stephanotis in the most romantic of bridal bouquets. Nor need hosta foliage take a back seat in bridal decor. Nora Fields, formerly of New York Botanic Garden, has, among others, fashioned hosta leaves into flower-form arrangements for use at weddings, as hand-held bouquets, corsages or integrated floral arrangements for the table.

The wonderful thing about such uses of hosta foliage is that it is not only impressive, but also can be

Table flower arrangement, by Nora Fields, utilizing hosta foliage. (Arrangement by Nora Fields)

readily employed by the novice. Employing hosta materials will become a key element in your arranging repertoire, once you have gained some experience with their splendid qualities.

Before proceeding, it should be noted that hostas have two other useful characteristics for flower arrangers. First, they are easy to grow, either in the ground or in pots. Second, the leaves, flowers and seeds are easily preserved by the silica-gel dessicant method (see background glossary), thus extending their usefulness indoors, especially during the winter season.

Some arrangements that I will propose and discuss are pure whimsy to stimulate the imagination of the viewer. Others are examples of basic concepts, suitable for individual tastes, homes and living styles. (See background glossary for Styles of Flower Arranging). A lesson plan for each arrangement will define the procedures, and serve as a guide to get you started. Soon, as you gain experience and become more aware of arrangements of form and color in nature, you can create your own "signature" for arrangements. Arranging plant materials can be an experience of gentle love, of care, of a form of civilized behavior to mark either special or everyday occasions in our lives, or special memories such as birthdays, anniversaries, or weddings, which gain an added and heightened dimension with flower arrangements. Even at sad occasions, plant materials serve to offer some comfort and to remind us that life goes on all around us and will be ours tomorrow.

It is understandable that flowers play an important role in our lives. Not only the existence of flowers and leaves in fossils, which give us some understanding of the changes of our planet, but their presence in the writings of the Bible, paintings and crafted ornaments indicate that flowers and leaves have always had a message to convey. The elegant French Louis styles, the sophisticated Empire style, as well as the tightly massed Victorian, the wonderful Colonial and Williamsburg styles, to the provocative Art Nouveau and Art Deco, all benefit from the use of hostas. One hesitates to use the term "universal" when referring to the value of a genus in various styles, yet hostas approach that standard in their potential use in arrangements.

The pictured arrangements, together with the lesson plans, will, I hope, stimulate you to discover the pleasure and satisfaction you can have in making arrangements in a great range of styles, whether they be Japanese Classical, Traditional, Naturalistic or Modern styles, including Ikenobo, Ohara and Sogetsu as taught by Ikebana schools (see background glossary for details). Each lesson plan will explain the philosophy and concept, as well as the method of arranging.

Components of previous arrangement used as hand-held bouquet. (Arrangement by Nora Fields)

Closeup of previous arrangement showing details of foliage flowers fashioned from *H.* 'Reversed' and *H.* 'Shade Fanfare' leaves. (Arrangement by Nora Fields)

Flower Arranging with Hostas

Dynasty Flowers (Arrangement by M. Herweg)   *Goddess of Mercy* (Arrangement by M. Herweg)

DYNASTY FLOWERS

In the manner of Chinese flower arranging (see background glossary)

Container: Chinese peach design porcelain

Materials and Order of Insertion:

    1. 1 stem, Uchida Lily

    2. 1 leaf, *Hosta* 'Shogun'

Arrangement Concepts:

    1. The Uchida Lily stem, consisting of a full flower and several buds is placed at about the same height as the container, with the full flower facing slightly to the front. The whole stem must be placed so that the emphasis is on the beauty of the line with the flower buds as both the foreground and background. In essence, the flowers create the illusion of "Cloud Formations." An asymmetrical balanced look is the objective.

    2. The hosta leaf is placed to slightly soften the container lip, yet part of the beauty is the graceful disappearance of the stem into the container. One or several species of plant materials may be used. The flowers and container must be compatible and share equal visual impact.

GODDESS OF MERCY

American Flower Arranging Style

Circular Silhouette—Mass-Line Design

Accessory as a feature

Container: Blue Japanese water basin

Accessory: Japanese antique porcelain Goddess of Mercy

Materials and Order of Insertion:

    1. Feature, Goddess of Mercy

    2. 5 leaves, *Hosta* 'Shogun'

    3. 3 flower stems, *Hosta* 'Fragrant Bouquet'

    4. The statue is placed in the center of the container, which is the height of the arrangement, giving a visual feature, weight and symmetrical balance. The repetition of the blue color and shiny texture of the statue and container creates rhythmic movement, emphasis and interest.

    5. The hosta leaves are placed at the lower half creating the visual circular area and adding mass and weight.

    6. One flower stalk is placed higher than the leaves as a line to give another point on the circle silhouette, and to increase movement from top to middle to the bottom of the design. The other 2 flower stalks are placed low to enhance the statue.

PROUD AS A PEACOCK

Art Nouveau
Vertical-Mass-Line Design
Container: Authentic Art Nouveau three-handled glass vase
Materials and Order of Insertion:

    1. 3 peacock feathers

    2. 1 green leaf, *Hosta* 'Fragrant One' (low in front)

    3. 1 yellow leaf, *Hosta* 'Shade Master' (tallest in back)

    4. 2 blue leaves, *Hosta* 'Blue Wedgwood' (in front above #2)

    5. 1 green leaf *Hosta*, 'Fragrant One' (slightly shorter and in back and in front of #2)

    6. 2 green leaves, *Hosta* 'Fall Bouquet' (in back and under #3)

    7. 2 yellow leaves, *Hosta* 'Shade Master' (in front sides)

    8. 1 green leaf, *Hosta* 'Fragrant One' (on right side)

In this vertical-mass-line style, the peacock feathers are used to create a tall, light and airy silhouette which establishes the line. The massing of the soft, muted yellows and greens of the hosta leaves at the bottom enhances and strengthens the line. The plant material is not much wider than the width of the vase. This vertical mass-line style was very popular, and arrangements were placed in many rooms of the home.

Proud as a Peacock (Arrangement by M. Herweg)

Pineapple—the Symbol of Hospitality (Arrangement by M. Herweg)

PINEAPPLE—THE SYMBOL OF HOSPITALITY

Modern Flower Arrangements
Modern Vertical Mass-Line Design
Container: Modern hand-made compote
Materials and Order of Insertion:

    1. Variegated pineapple

    2. 2 variegated dark-green edged leaves, *Hosta* 'Reversed' (low and in front)

    3. 1 large variegated leaf, *Hosta* 'Vicki Aden' (tallest in back)

    4. 1 large dark blue leaf, *Hosta* 'Blue Umbrellas' (in front and above #2)

    5. 1 cream-edged leaf, *Hosta* 'Snow Cap' (in front and above #4)

    6. 1 green-edged leaf, *Hosta* 'Reversed' (above #5)

Flower Arranging with Hostas

HOSTAS IN SUMMER GLORY

Ikenobo School of Ikebana
Nishu-ike Shoka—2 Material arrangement:
Container: Lotus leaf-shaped ceramic
Material and Order of Insertion:
1. Tall flower stalk
2. Tallest back leaf
3. Front facing leaf
4. Short front flower stalk
5. Short front leaf
6. Short variegated *Tovara* leaves on right front
7. Tall variegated *Tovara* leaves on left back
Number 1, 2, 3, 4, 5—*Hosta* 'Fragrant Candelabra'
Number 6, 7—*Tovara*
Arrangement Concepts:
1. Shin: The flower stalk has been used very tall because of the hosta growth habit. Shin is set according to the style of the pattern of the plant material.
2. Soe: The leaf is about 3/5 of the length of Shin, and placed on the right, back side of Shin, which is also a change from the basic pattern.
3. Tai helper: This leaf is a transition between Shin and Tai, and faces Tai.
4. Tai helper: This must be a flower stalk in bud only, as it is used low in the leaf grouping.
5. Tai: ¾ of Soe length. This leaf is low, slightly on the right, front side, and faces up to Shin. Thus essentially creating a clump of hostas growing in nature, while still confirming the rules of Shoka placement.
6. This stem of a variegated leaf of woody material is placed low to give the visual impression that it is growing through the hosta. It is on the right side, under the Soe leaf.
7. This stem of a variegated leaf of woody material is placed high and to the left back. The combination of woody and grass (flowers) materials have been combined to achieve a natural Shoka style. Small, water-smoothed pebbles are placed in the container to cover the needle-holder.

TROPICAL NIGHTS

Ikenobo School of Ikebana
Jiyuku Style-Modern Free Style
Container: Japanese Iwata green glass compote
Materials and Order of Insertion:
1. 1 leaf, *Hosta* 'Blue Umbrellas'
2. 1 short red Anthurium

Hostas in Summer Glory (Arrangement by M. Herweg)

Tropical Nights (Arrangement by M. Herweg)

3. 1 tall red Anthurium

4. 3 red lacquer boards

In Modern Free Style, the aim of the arranger is to create something new and exciting. Thus, the large hosta leaf has been cut along the veins (ribs) to remove the center portion, so as to delete any sense of a natural look.

Arrangement Concepts:

1. The hosta leaf is placed low, just over the edge of the vase to give a continuous line. The front of the leaf shows the prominent veins (ribs) and carries the eye up and back, featuring the cut-out void area.

2. The short anthurium gives strong basal balance.

3. The placement of the tall anthurium on the central visual axil line lifts and carries the design visually to lofty heights.

4. The uneven placement of the lacquer boards adds the drama needed, as well as providing the interlayering of red (boards), green (container), red (tall Anthurium). All the components used are needed to give this arrangement its sense of modern style.

An Autumn Garden (Arrangement by M. Herweg)

AN AUTUMN GARDEN

Ohara School of Ikebana
Rimpa Style
Container: Japanese Oribe Suiban
Accessory: Natural weathered wooden stand
Materials and Order of Insertion:

1. Bloomstock, *Hosta* 'Fragrant Candelabra' (tallest)

2. 3 stems of striped grass, *Miscanthus sinensis* 'Cabaret'

3. 5 stems, *Miscanthus sinensis* 'Strictus'

4. 3 leaves cream-edged, variegated leaves, 1 *Hosta* 'Shogun', 2 *Hosta* 'Wide Brim'

5. 2 large, green leaves, *Hosta* 'Green Wedge', 1 leaf, *Hosta* 'Blue Umbrellas'

6. 5 pampas grass flower plumes

7. 3 stems hydrangea

8. 2 seed stalks fennel

9. 3 stems small yellow chrysanthemums

Arrangement Concepts:

1. Establish the tallest height—maybe Ki (woody) or Kusa (grass) plant material

2–3. Establish the middle and lower areas, and width, foreground and depth.

4–5. Visually and actually reinforce the 2–3 lines, using the lighter colorations in the front, with darker in back.

6. By using the flower plumes of Miscanthus, a season theme is established.

7–8–9. Large and small forms are added for natural growth contrast. The Oribe container was especially chosen and photographed at a slight angle to reinforce the folding of the screen panels. Your artistic eye should now envision and expand this into a magnificent 12 folding-panel screen.

BOYHOOD MEMORIES One Iris—One Son

Ohara School of Ikebana
Small Form Style A.
Container: Ohara small form compote
Materials and Order of Insertion:

1. 1 blue iris

2. 2 leaves, *Hosta* 'Vicki Aden'

Arrangement Concepts:

1. Subject: The blue iris is placed so the leaves give a feeling of foreground and slight natural depth.

2. Object: The hosta leaf is placed low, almost in front.

3. Filler: The second hosta leaf is placed as a

visual transition, and to give weight to balance the tall iris. The aim of this pattern is to express the beauty of flowers and branches which rise vertically from the center of the container.

In Japan, the iris is the flower used for Boy's Day (celebrated May 5th). A bright paper or cloth fish (carp) banner is flown atop a bamboo pole for each boy of the family. A flower arrangement featuring iris is usually on display along with a collection of samurai swords and armor.

Boyhood Memories (Arrangement by M. Herweg)

THREE CALLAS IN A ROW

Ohara School of Ikebana
The One Row Style
Container: Multi-color, tube-like ceramic
Materials and Order of Insertion:
    1. 2 tall yellow Calla Lilies
    2. 2 shorter yellow Calla Lilies
    3. 1 leaf on left side, *Hosta* 'Reversed'
    4. 1 leaf on right side, *Hosta* 'Wide Brim'
    5. 5 tall leaves on left and right sides, *Yucca filamentosa* 'Color Guard'
    6. 1 tall leaf, *Yucca filamentosa* 'Color Guard' behind shorter Calla
    7. 2 crossed leaves, *Yucca filamentosa* 'Aureo-marginata'
Arrangement Concepts:
    1. Subject: The calla on the left side as per picture. The secondary calla on the right side, the height is the same as the subject for visual impact, repetition and a non-realistic look.
    2. Object: The height to achieve balance between top and bottom of the arrangement.
    3–4. Subject and secondary fillers: Set at the same height to strengthen the impact of the 2 main lines.
    5–6. Fillers: To soften and carry the eye down.
    7. Fillers: Crossed to further develop the modern concept.

Three Callas in a Row (Arrangement by M. Herweg)

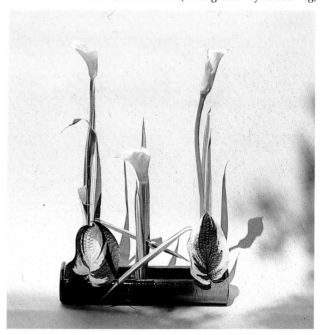

Romantic Victorian (Arrangement by M. Herweg)

ROMANTIC VICTORIAN

European Flower Arranging Style
Early Victorian Period (1830–1850)
Oval Silhouette-Mass Design
Container: Antique Victorian alabaster urn
Materials and Order of Insertion:

1. 7 stems, variegated grass, *Miscanthus sinensis* 'Cabaret'
2. 9 stems, miniature white gladiolus
3. 7 variegated leaves at container lip, *Hosta* 'White Magic', *Hosta* 'Reversed'
4. 5 white flower stalks, *Hosta* 'Fragrant Bouquet'
5. 15 white starburst chrysanthemums
6. 25 small white roses
7. 4 variegated leaves, *Hosta fluctuans* 'Variegated', cut in half

Arrangement Concepts:

1. As you begin this arrangement, use the 7 stems of the variegated grass to establish the height and the sides of the silhouette.
2. Place the white gladiolus to further reinforce the lines, and to add some actual and visual weight.
3. Place the 7 variegated hosta leaves at the lip of the vase to soften and give bottom weight and stability.
4. The 5 large white hosta flower stalks again add weight, and a large flower mass-line form.
5. The 15 white chrysanthemums are placed to fill in void areas, with no regard to establishing a visual rhythm.
6. The 25 small garden roses are again placed as above.
7. To bring the eye up into the middle of the arrangement, 4 large variegated hosta leaves are placed at the middle area. As these leaves are so large, they were cut in half, and tucked into the other flower forms.

WISTERIA VINES IN AUTUMN

Sogetsu School of Ikebana
Nageire Style—Hanging Style
Variation No. 4—Hanging Free Style
Container: Green and white ceramic
Materials and Order of Insertion:

1. 1 wisteria vine
2. 2 leaves, *Hosta* 'Paul Aden'
3. 2 stems, yellow Fuji mums

Arrangement Concepts:

1. Shin or Main Line: The wisteria vine is twisted and invisibly tied to achieve weight balance below and above the container, as this is the natural growth tendency. It creates a vine in autumn and gives great importance to the open circular areas and the fewer green leaves.
2. Hikae line: The two hosta leaves are placed to cover the top of the container, and provide height and background.
3. Jushi or helpers: The two stems of mums give a visual transition and textural contrast to the rough vines and smooth hosta leaves.

A garden effect has been achieved by the natural use and placement of plant material.

Wisteria Vines in Autumn (Arrangement by M. Herweg)

A Garden Scene (Arrangement by M. Herweg)

A GARDEN SCENE

European Gardenesque Style
Container: Hand-woven reed-handled basket
Materials and Order of Insertion:
1. Bloomstock (tallest), *Hosta* 'Fragrant Candelabra'
2. 5 cream-edged leaves, *Hosta* 'Fragrant Bouquet', 5 small green-edged yellow leaves, *Hosta* 'Just So'
3. Tall violet flower stocks
4. 3 blue-green leaves, *Hosta* 'Fall Bouquet' (left side)
5. 3 lavender bloomstocks, *Hosta* 'Fall Bouquet' (left side)
6. 3 white bloomstocks, *Hosta* 'Fragrant Bouquet' (right side)
7. 3 stems, yellow goldenrod
8. 1 stem, purple chrysanthemum
9. 1 bloomstock, Turtlehead
10. 2 stems, small white chrysanthemums
11. 2 orange seed stems
12. 2 seed stocks, *Hosta*.

BACKGROUND GLOSSARY

Design Elements of Flower Arranging

A writer cannot get very far in discussing flower arranging without touching upon design elements, or the planned visual arrangement of the physical components used. Design brings order to a flower arrangement, as it does to any other art medium. Flower arranging is simply an art form, which, guided by the principles of design, focuses on plant materials as the medium.

A short review of the seven elements, with which the practice of design is concerned, may prove helpful:

1. **Space** refers to the total space, spaces within the plant material, other components, and also includes the unoccupied spaces within the design, so space is concerned with the three-dimensional organization of the arrangement.

2. **Line** is almost exclusively one-dimensional, a communicating relationship that leads the eye easily through the design along the planned visual paths.

3. **Form** deals with the three-dimensional qualities of the plant and other material used, whether it be closed or open, regular or irregular. The term is applied both to the shape of the individual components as well as the entire arrangement.

4. **Size** deals with the apparent and visual size of the arrangement and is a function of its line, shape, form and space, as well as its color(s), texture(s) and pattern(s). The placement of the arrangement, relative to the viewer, is a critical factor in the sense of size, as the closer the arrangement is to the viewer, the larger it will appear to be, as it occupies a larger proportion of the visual space seen by the eye.

5. **Color** deals with the viewer's response to the light rays reflected from the arrangement. Whenever practical, the flower arranger should attempt to use lighting (natural or artificial) and colors that conform to the color palette found in nature. A practical understanding of how people react to the various colors as well as the moods they create is an important element in the arranger's body of design skills.

6. **Texture** adds interest as an additional variation that stimulates our visual and touch response to the surface finish of the materials used, such as its roughness, smoothness, dullness, shine, etc. The texture must harmonize with the background, the container, the accessories as well as the other plant materials used. Textures can modify our perception of form, color and size, while adding interest and variety, but must be used with restraint, in keeping with the total theme of the arrangement.

7. **Pattern** refers to the silhouette created by the combination of lines, forms, colors and the spaces

between them. Together the plant materials as arranged in the container along with the other components, form the pattern or silhouette of the finished design.

Pigment System of Color

Unlike paint artists, flower arrangers do not mix colors to create new ones, but some knowledge of the *Pigment System of Color*, which divides the 12 hues into a color wheel, is helpful. The color wheel includes:

1. The three primary colors—red and yellow (both warm) as well as blue (cool). With these primaries, all of the other colors can be created.

2. The three secondary colors—*orange* is produced by mixing equal amounts of red and yellow, *green* is created by mixing equal amounts of yellow and blue, *violet* is produced by mixing equal amounts of blue and red.

3. The intermediate colors: achieved by mixing equal amounts of primary and secondary colors, resulting in orange-red as well as yellow-orange, yellow-green, blue-green, blue-violet and red-violet.

4. The neutral colors—black (the absence of color), white (the inclusion of all the colors) and gray (a mixture of white and black), none of which are hues. However, when hues are mixed with neutrals, a wide variety of exciting shades, tints and tones can be created.

The *Pigment System of Color*, as presented on a color wheel, can be applied to the choice of plant materials. For example, colors that are too close may not complement each other. The color wheel also helps in determining the relative impact of colors— for example, pure colors have a greater impact (and thus may "clash" more readily) than those mixed with whites or blacks, and the relationships between the colors chosen.

Preserving Plant Materials

Great success can be achieved in drying leaves, flowers, seeds and berries by the desiccant method, so your beautiful garden flowers can be preserved for a long-lasting, dried bouquet. There are three general types of desiccants, all of which can be used over and over again:

1. **Silica Gel:** The most expensive, but the quickest and most effective. In its dry form, it is bluish in color and must be stored in an air-tight container. It becomes whitish or pink in color when it has absorbed moisture from the plant material being dried. It can then be dried in an oven at 225°F (107°C) until it changes back to blue, making it reuseable.

2. **Borax, Cornmeal, and Builder's Sand:** Equal parts of these ingredients, thoroughly mixed, will dry the larger sizes and not so fragile plant material. This combination takes a longer time than silica-gel, but can be dried and reused as above.

3. **Kitty Litter** (non-chlorophyll type): While the least expensive, it will leave a slight, powdery film on some plant material, which may be brushed off with a soft bristle brush. Since the particles are large, it is only used for larger plant material, or berries, and may also be dried and reused as above in #1.

Regardless of which desiccant is used, the purpose for quick drying is to stop the growth process, so color, shape and form are preserved. Stems of most flowers do not dry well, so cut the stems off, leaving only an inch attached to each flower head. It is preferable to then attach a few inches of fine wire to each flower. The wire can be run through the calyx sideways and twisted back on itself, or thrust through the center of the flowerhead and bent to form a hook that can be hidden in the flower's center. Another method is to dip the wire in glue and push it into the remaining inch of stem. After the flowers are dried, larger pieces of wire may be added for whatever length is needed for arranging. This wire stem should be covered with corsage tape.

Any air-tight container may be used for drying. Place a thin layer of desiccant on the bottom, then place the flowers, not touching each other, on the desiccant. Then, carefully cover the flowers with about 1 in. (2.5 cm) of the dessicant, making sure the petals, sepals, calyxes, stamens, and pistils are supported in natural positions. Place only the same size flowers in a single container, so that they will require the same drying time. Cover the container and allow to dry from 2 days to 2 weeks, until the plant material is completely dry. Check carefully as to proper drying. Overdrying makes plant material too brittle and natural color is lost.

After the plant material is dried, and the wire stems are taped, then arrange them in any appropriate style. Usually, mass-type arrangements are best for dried material. Adding some dried foliage or grasses, ferns or seed pods gives a more natural look. Hosta seed stems dry particularly well, and look lovely. To aid plant material, so that they will not be so fragile, as well as sealing against moisture, lightly spray with lacquer, varnish or flower spray. Do not use hair spray, as it attracts dust, moisture and becomes messy. Remember, it takes much more dried material than fresh material to look well, so dry enough to ensure an ample supply and choices when beginning to arrange.

Rules of Flower Arranging

Like other forms of art, flower arranging has developed rules that are based on centuries of experience as to what appeals to people. Think of the elements and principles of design as called out in the traditional and period styles as helpful guides, as basic formulas to get started. There is always an interplay between the plant materials and the design as to which will dominate, and to what degree. There are six principles of design, which apply to flower arranging as well as other forms of art. They seem to be based on how humans react to elements in their environment. More importantly, they work in executing flower arrangements. A brief description of the design principles follows:

1. **Balance** achieves visual stability by placing equal weight on opposite sides of an imaginary axis and should be evident from all sides. The axis is always vertical because balance is related to the force of gravity. Symmetrical balance is repetition of all elements, including space, on each side of the central axis with both sides being as nearly alike as possible. Asymmetric balance is achieved by equalizing visual weight, even if composed of different elements in varying directions with unequal space about the axis. Visual weight differs from actual weight. Denser, bolder forms, and larger sizes, as well as darker colors and coarser textures appear heavier. Their opposites appear lighter in weight. Asymmetrical balance has greater appeal aesthetically than symmetrical balance, but is more difficult to attain, as greater judgment is involved.

2. **Proportion** deals with the relationship of areas and the relative amounts to each other and the whole. It is the relative length of a line, as well as the relative area value in form or space. It is an amount, but not a size comparison. Good proportion is the variation of one form, part, or color to another, or to the whole. The "golden mean," i.e., the ratio of 1 to 1.6, is pleasing to most people as they observe art forms and serves as a good guide for the beginner.

3. **Scale** refers to the size relations of the component parts of a design. Repetition, variation, and contrast of size must be in good scale. When contrast of size is too great, the components are out of scale.

4. **Rhythm** refers to a dominant, visual path through the design which suggests motion, and gives a design a sense of being alive, rather than at rest. It may be achieved by repetition or gradations of line, form, space, size, color, texture, and flower patterns. Successful design moves by easy gradation from solidity to thinness or delicacy at the extremities.

5. **Dominance** refers to the greater force of one kind of element or plant material, relative to other elements which are subordinated. Dominance is achieved by the use and placement of space, line, form, size, color and texture. It helps to determine the main theme.

6. **Contrast** is achieved by placing opposite or unlike elements together to emphasize difference. Contrast exists only between elements arranged together to emphasize difference. Contrast exists only between elements that are related in some manner, such as contrasts of line, form, space, size, color, and texture. Restraint should be used as too much contrast using too many elements results in confusion.

Styles of Flower Arranging

A brief primer on the styles of flower arranging can give some insight into and increase an understanding of the actual examples of arrangements illustrated and discussed. In *naturalistic* styles, mother nature is the master, and plant materials are arranged as they grew in nature. In *classical* and *traditional* styles, while a very precise pattern of arranging the plant material is prescribed, the arranger is the master of mother nature. In *modern* styles, the plant materials serve as an art medium with the elements and principles of design as the master. Further detailed, background material on the styles of flower arranging includes:

1. **Chinese Style,** as exampled by *Dynasty Flowers*, was colorful, gay and life-like with few rigid rules or restraints, and was considered an integral part of a home's interior decoration to be exhibited in harmony with everyday surroundings. Much emphasis was placed on the understanding and appreciation of merits and virtues possessed by specific flowers. Some flowers are noted for special qualities, such as distinct beauty or symbols of significant spiritual or ethical values. Another feature is the discriminate selection of flowers and containers and accessories or complementary objects such as carved semiprecious stone, or ceramic pieces of fruit, small folding screens, cloisonne animals or birds, small, rare or old books and sometimes a small potted plant. This vignette grouping was usually staged on a handsome, carved flower stand. In addition to the elements themselves, admiration of the beauty and elegance of a well-designed arrangement, emphasis is on the appreciation of line and balance, and is equivalent to a composition in a painting with the principles of design and balance skillfully executed. The highly developed craft of porcelain and design motifs has contributed a distinct style to Chinese floral art. Today, dynasty flowers are no longer arranged, yet they are being recreated in paintings, scrolls, fabrics and porcelains. The peach, also known as the "fairy" fruit, appears in many Chinese art

forms, as it appeals to the aesthetic sense of the people. It is an emblem of marriage, as well as a symbol of immortality and springtime. The sacred peach tree of the immortals was said to blossom once in 3,000 years, and to yield the fruit of immortality, which ripened for another 3,000 years. An old man, the God of Longevity, is often depicted emerging from a peach. The peach was the first fruit offered to Buddha as a baby.

2. **American,** as exampled by *Goddess of Mercy,* features a pattern or silhouette in a geometric shape, and the placement of plant material and objects must be contained within that imaginary or real area. The statue is used as a feature which is anything in an arrangement in addition to the plant material, whether it be a container, base, mechanics or background which is dominant in a design. The statue establishes the height diameter of the circle, and the leaves are placed to establish the side diameter. In a mass-line design, the plant material enhances and strengthens the line, and the silhouette is open.

Art Nouveau Style, as exampled by *Proud as a Peacock,* emerged at the end of the 19th Century as an original concept which discarded the styles of the past. The Japanese influence was very marked and resulted in the naturalistic replication of flower, trees and animals. Simplicity of line and forms coupled with soft and muted colors were typical. This style influenced not only art, but interior and exterior decorations, and even jewelry. The Art Nouveau style greatly influenced not only the arranging of flowers, but also the containers, which required handmade-appearing pottery (preferred over porcelain), opaque glass of muted colors and dull metals. Grueby and Rookwood pottery, Tiffany, and Lalique glass wares were much prized. Ancient glass unearthed in Syria, Egypt and Rome, with peacock blues, violets, and greens were the accepted color preference.

Flowers were sometimes arranged like an open fan with the stems all of the same height, and often half as high as the vase. Naturally tall flowers or branches were often arranged at twice the height of the vase, but never to look heavy.

Modern Style, as exampled by *Pineapple—the Symbol of Hospitality,* following the Art Nouveau and Art Deco Periods, emerged in the 1930s as a new artistic style which involved a blending of the styles of all earlier periods, but with emphasis on natural or abstract beauty. Color, form, unity, rhythm and balance were the important elements and principles of design. Line arrangements were preferred using geometric shapes with bold silhouettes. Distinctive and unusual plant material, combinations of fruits and vegetables with other plant material, and even

painted wood and plant material were used. Bold, rich colors were now preferred to pastels. Modern or abstract style vases were designed using glass, pottery, wood or metal. This modern style of flower arrangement remains a changing and growing style. In modern arrangements, the height of the plant material is the same as the width of the vase. So, for example, the pineapple and hosta leaves are placed in the center of the vase in a vertical line shape of an inverted "T." To balance the heavy visual and actual weight of the pineapple, the hosta leaves are massed and placed lower, continuing the line of the vase. The pineapple in our Colonial Williamsburg Period became the symbol of hospitality and was frequently used in decorations. The style of placing the pineapple at the top of the design borrows from the 17th and 18th Century Dutch and Flemish Periods when it was the practice to place a large lily or fritillaria at the very top. The combined plant material is used in a dramatic and exotic manner, with a strong upright, bold silhouette. Unnecessary and confusing visual details are eliminated, using the plant material in a sculptural manner.

3. **European**

Variations of European Style

Gardenesque Style, as exampled by *A Garden Scene,* inspired by the Japanese Naturalistic style, simulates the plants of four gardens. The arranging area is divided into four equal areas: left side (back and front) and right side (back and front). The plant material on the left side must balance the plant material of the right side, yet the silhouette space areas must be unequal, as in an informal garden. As no two gardens are arranged in exactly the same way and only a few flowers of each kind are used to give the sense of the vastness of nature, colors on each side must be different (even discordant), just as some gardens are planted with tall flowers and other gardens with shorter flowers together with different trees and shrubs. Essentially, use plant material as it grew, yet aim for a unified view that visually completes the four gardens as a whole composition.

Victorian Style, as exampled by *Romantic Victorian,* is characterized by an overlapping of the classicism of the late Georgian and Regency, and the light in form and color, airy oval masses of Louis XVI. White, cream and light tints of pink, lavender and yellow were combined to demonstrate the grace and profusion of the flowers. Large and small flowers were used together with little sense of scale or proportion and no center of interest, but with flowers placed to best show off their unique beauty. Some of the stems were visible as they disappeared into the vase. The overall height of the arrangement was from 1–2 times the height of the vase, creating a lovely oval silhouette. Vases were Belleck, Ironstone or Haviland China, Parian Ware, glass lustre and many new types and colors of Victorian glass. Silver and gold gilt were also much favored, as were alabaster urns. Vase shapes included urns, pitchers, tureens, baskets, and many whimsical shapes such as hands, cornucopias, shoes, etc. From the 1850s to the end of her reign, Victoria's preference for dark colors from the blues to purples to magentas became the popular colors. The oval design became round, only as tall or shorter than the vase, and with a tight massing of flowers. Small, "tussy-mussy" bouquets using the "Language of Flowers," became popular and books were written explaining the combinations of flowers and the message of love they conveyed.

4. Japanese

Ikebana Style: Ikebana means "living flowers." When Buddhism was introduced into Japan from India and China in the 7th Century, the Buddhist monks placed live flowers on the altars at Nara, and institutionalized the Japanese love of flowers. In the 7th Century, Ono-no-Imako, an envoy to the Imperial Court of China, upon returning to Japan, retired to his house and garden by a pond (Ike-no-bo) to devote the rest of his life to the development of Ikebana for the Buddhist temples. Ikebana, or Japanese Style flower arranging has become an integral part of the Japanese culture. For 13 centuries, the Japanese have studied, observed and experimented with the art of flower arranging. There are today many distinct schools teaching Ikebana.

Variation of Ikebana Style:

Ohara School: One of the most popular of the Ikebanai Schools, which was founded in the 1890s created a new style of naturalistic flower arranging in low flat containers. *Moribana* means "piled up flowers," an indication of the style first used by Unshin Ohara, the founder of the Ohara School. *Moribana* techniques are now taught by most schools of Ikebana. By fashioning the container after low bonsai pots and using a circular lead-holder to hold the flower stems, the aim of creating a low, flat, naturalistic flower arrangement is realized. Houn Ohara is the present Headmaster and grandson of the founder.

Ohara School Style Variations

Small Form Arrangement, as exampled by *Boyhood Memories,* was created in 1973. This is a smaller, less expensive and easier style to learn and create, and more suitable for smaller homes. As there are only 2 main lines, and the role of the fillers become more important; however, there is no fixed rule governing their placement. Fillers can be used freely to express one's individual feelings and imagination. The characteristics of this style are the simplicity of construction, as well as the beauty of the colors of the flowers.

One Row Style, as exampled by *Three Callas in a Row,* was introduced in 1973, and is a more advanced technique which gives a great deal of freedom from the prior, more rigid rules. The container must be long and narrow and the branches are placed in a row, side by side to form the framework with essentially no foreground or depth. The length of the subject stem is prescribed, but the lengths of the secondary and object stems are determined by artistic and design skill, and to express harmony and perspective. The use of fillers is quite free and may be placed outside the boundary of the three main branches. Because the length of the fillers is not fixed, they must be determined with balance in mind. Usually, the subject and secondary lines are the same material; however, as one progresses in learning, the material choices are left more to the discretion of the arranger. The base of the arrangement (water's edge) can be seen clearly, and must be tidy, and with a very shallow depth.

Rimpa Style, as exampled by *An Autumn Garden,* emerged in the 1970s, using the techniques and beauty of the antique Japanese folding screens of the 16th and 17th centuries on which wonderful flower gardens were painted. However, on a screen, these gardens had visually little or no foreground or depth and appeared quite flat due to the painting techniques. Thus the plant materials placed in the Rimpa Style have little depth or foreground and the plant material barely extends over the front or back edges of the container. A profusion of many tree, shrub and flower materials are used, creating an illusion of the vastness of nature, yet the restraint of a garden exists. Only a few of each kind of plant material are used. Specific Heaven-Man-Earth line relationships are not apparent, yet there must be different height levels, as you are creating the total existence of a garden. Large and small flowers, dark and light colors, sparse and full-leaved or flowered branches, and irregular and regular shapes and forms are mingled to achieve a wholly natural garden design. There must be open spaces in the arrangement, and plant material must be used as it grows, with a great respect for the 4 seasons of nature.

Ikenobo School, as exampled by *Hostas in Summer Glory,* is the oldest and most traditional school of Japanese flower arranging for pleasure, dating from the 15th Century.

Variations of Ikenobo Style

Rikka Style means "standing up plant cutting," and is a highly demanding technique requiring at least nine (9) flowers and branch placements. Most other Ikenobo styles are derived from this concept.

There are three traditional styles of simplified Rikka called Shoka, using respectively 1, 2 or 3 types of plant material.

Shoka Style, as exampled by *Hostas in Summer Glory,* is a series of contrived, disciplined patterns involving the use of 1, 2 or 3 plant materials. Hosta leaves and flower stalks here are arranged according to many prescribed rules and patterns, enhancing their natural beauty of growth. In the Shoka arrangement, the hosta leaves and flower stalks have been used with the lengths changed from the basic pattern. The varying stem lengths are referred to as the Shin-Soe-Tai.

Modern Free Style, as exampled by *Tropical Nights,* has the aim of creating something new and exciting. Thus, the large hosta leaf has been cut along the veins (ribs) to remove the center portion, so as to deny any sense of a natural look. The new free-style Shoka is called Shin-pu-tai. Sen-ei Ikenobo, the 45th lineal descendant of the founder, is the present Headmaster of the Ikenobo School.

Ikebana became very rigid during the 200-year rule of the Tokugawa feudal government. With the opening of Japan to the West in 1854, a great introduction of new plant materials and flower styles led to radical new departures in arranging styles.

Sogetsu School, as exampled by *Wisteria Vines in Autumn,* was founded in the 1920s by Sofu Teshigahara, known as the "Picasso of Flower Arrangement." He rebelled against the rigid rules of classical Ikebana, wanting to use plant material to interpret the elements and principles of design in a more visual art form. The name Sogetsu means "moon," and "grass," and suggests a deep feeling for nature, plus a deep appreciation for the vastness of the universe. The three main principles advocated by the Sogetsu School are that 1) anyone can arrange flowers; 2) arrangements can be displayed anywhere; and 3) any material can be used. Sofu is considered the "Father of Modern Ikebana." Hiroshi Teshigahara is the son of the founder and now present headmaster.

Nageire Style, as exampled by *Wisteria Vines in Autumn,* places importance on choosing plant materials so that hanging or cascading lines look natural and not contrived or forced. The top lip of the container must be broken or covered by material so that the completed arrangement appears as a whole composition. The stems of all plant materials are either held by sticks placed inside the container mouth, or are rested against the inside, the latter method is used here.

In one class conducted by Sofu, he stated, "If there were just one hour to create a flower arrangement, spend forty minutes becoming familiar with the plant material, then in the remaining twenty minutes, a beautiful Ikebana could be created." Each time I am with flowers, I appreciate this statement more, and continue to understand man's communication with nature.

A simple, yet elegant arangement, using *H.* "Wide Brim" leaves. (Arrangement by Nora Fields)

VII

HAROLD EPSTEIN

Small Hostas in Difficult Places

The charm and beauty of the smaller members of many families of flowers have recently been more frequently recognized; and not only because they suit the smaller garden better. They have in themselves a grace and a quality, a freshness and a charm, not due merely to their diminutive size, and often missing in their larger counterparts—Despite the grandeur and magnificence of the finest of the larger specimens, many more among the smaller representatives of the genus equal and indeed excel their bigger brothers in their form and habit, in their colour and quality.[1]

This reference to the *Rhododendron* genus is equally relevant to the *Hosta* genus, the use of which has increased in popularity tremendously in recent years. Their hardiness, durability, usefulness and ease of culture in the garden accounts for their ready acceptance. But with the continual shrinking of home gardens, there is a corresponding need for less space-consuming plants. This limitation of garden area especially applies to the Japanese gardener. His (her) greatest problem is adequate living space. Small spaces limit the ability to cultivate large numbers of plants. Small spaces result in a preference for small species and the use of pot culture.

H. tortifrons

Japan is the primary source of *Hosta* species. A number of the small species have been in cultivation in Japan for centuries. By cultivation, I mean that potted Hostas are seen in temples, shrines, stores, on sidewalks, verandas, living rooms as well as gardens. Many of these same hostas (without the pots) are gradually being introduced into and cultivated in the Occident. The most common are *Hosta gracillima, lancifolia, tardiflora, tortifrons* and *venusta*.

Some of the choicest, recent, small *Hosta* immigrants from Japan have been variegated. There are also some newcomers from Japan with questionable names.

---

[1]Quoted from "Forward" by Lord Aberconway, President of the Royal Horticultural Society in *Dwarf Rhododendrons* by Peter A. Cox (1973).

Some small hostas, under evaluation, in a rock garden setting. Sempervivens in flower.

It cannot be assumed that because Japan is the source of a hosta that their names are correct. In the last two decades, there has been a tremendous spurt, not only in interest in, but in the number of available small hostas. The newer plants are the result of increased exploration, hybridizing and the use of radiation and chemical-mutagen techniques. The range of colors, forms, leaf-shapes and variegation patterns of the available small hostas today presents many new options to an old rock gardener like myself. There are interesting variations of blues, yellows, and multiple color combinations of yellows, whites and greens. The surprising thing is that these smaller hostas, when in clump strength are like lichens, they succeed where you least expect them to. They retain the stamina, the longevity, the ruggedness as well as the beauty of the larger, space-consuming hostas.

A viewing of the *Hosta* registrations with the International Registrar yields some interesting conclusions. From 1968 thru 1983 (16 years), 336 hosta cultivars were registered. From 1979 thru 1983 (5 years), 173 hosta cultivars were registered. At least 10% of those registered could be classified as SMALL. By SMALL, I mean that a single rosette is 8 in. (20 cm) high or less. Of course this may vary with culture. As the size of hostas determines to a large degree how they are used, and the number of plants required either for a square yard or a linear yard, it would be most helpful if catalogs offering hostas paid more attention to these details. I personally have either seen or used at least 30 different SMALL hostas— quite a selection.

As you may know, Japan has many shaded, rocky outcrops—the main reason that flat, open, arable land is so expensive in those islands. Hostas grow in those outcrops, in what seem to be perilous conditions. The rocky slopes are often sheer—save for a few Hosta plants hanging on in what could only be described as inhospitable crevices, often not enough for a toehold. Small hostas are often seen between tree roots where the soil could at best be called scant. This may be the perfect introduction to a discussion on small hosta roots. As evident from their performance, they must be long, penetrating roots and have excellent water-holding and gathering powers.

The rocky outcrops in Japan are not too different from those in many of our gardens—either natural or man-made. It is obviously easier to fit a plant into a difficult site, when it grows in that kind of site to begin with. These small hostas will probably appear even smaller under austere conditions. What's nice about them is that they are dependable and don't require constant coddling, the requisite recipe for success with many alpine plants in our home gardens.

Self-sown seedlings growing on rocky outcrop in Japan.

Some of those dark corners take on a new life with the use of yellow hostas, or any that have yellow or white in their variegation. It may take some experimentation, but you can find one or more small hostas that will do well under fairly dry conditions and others that will do well under almost constantly moist conditions. There are even a few which will adapt to either end of the range.

Let me share with you my experiences in trying to solve some rather difficult problems in my garden. I might start out by saying that my garden is in the northeastern United States with summer temperatures sometimes over 100°F (38°C) and winter

Tree stump used as a flower pot. Shown are *H. hypoleuca,* Polygonatum and Symphytum. Spiraea flowers in background.

temperatures sometimes down to −15°F (−26°C). But those temperature extremes are the smallest part of my problem. My main garden problem is that the glaciers 20,000 years ago left some of the biggest rocks you have ever seen. What soil there is, is rather poor. Yes, we have many rocky outcrops, just like Japan. 50 years ago, we did extensive dynamiting in the rocks so that we would have more places to tuck some plants in. We have gained the reputation down through the years of managing one of the most consistent graveyards for plants. Yet, we have had our successes and we have learned along the way.

Let me start out with a problem that we probably share—tree stumps. There comes a time when trees have trouble standing tall. It could be age. It could be the compaction of soil above the roots. It could be an assortment of insects, fungi or viruses, or the tree and the wind were not moving in the same direction at the same time and the resiliency was gone. Getting rid of the fallen trunk and branches is one thing, doing something with the stump is usually more difficult and potentially damaging to nearby plants. The idea of converting an ugly stump into something like

a huge flower pot was the original thought. It wasn't hard at all. In the fall, we dumped lots of leaves on top of the stump. The following spring we shoveled some soil on top of the wet leaves and then planted some small hostas together with a few Bergenia and Solomon Seal. Our new, big flower pot (alias tree stump) looks better as the years go by. In a way, it's a welcome change of pace to be able to see beautiful plants at close to eye level.

Another problem area developed around the base of a 35 year old Dawn Redwood (*Metasequoia glyptostroboides*). The tree is now about 90 ft. (27 m) high. The lawn that had originally grown up to the base of the trunk is gone, replaced by a mass of gnarled, tree roots. I had seen small hostas growing between similar roots in Japan. We mixed the little soil between the tree roots with leaf mold, sand and peat moss in roughly equal amounts. We set some small hostas along with some Japanese Painted Ferns (*Athyrium nipponicum*) in those pockets. We even set some small hostas in the deep pockets of the bronze colored trunk. We did favor the plants the first summer by watering so that they could establish themselves. Years have gone by and the setting still manages some very favorable comments from visitors.

Huge, bare boulders have a problem. They just look too bare, too sterile. Again, we tried small hostas, wherever we could find a crack, to squeeze in some soil and a small plant. Early spring plantings worked best. I'm not sure what the roots of the hostas will eventually do to the rocks. Please note the thing I feel may have the upper hand. In some ways, these efforts are artistic. The use of different colored hostas with different textures and forms may not replace the "pet rock", but the result is certainly easier to look at.

We had a few, very steep slopes where soil erosion was a serious problem. Many of the small hostas are stoloniferous, so we knew that they would eventually bind the soil. We set plants in clump size only about 6 in. (15 cm) apart and allowed them to grow for two years. From the increase, we were able to set plant divisions in clump strength (again in early spring) into the adjacent areas. Over a period of six years, we were able to reduce soil erosion to near zero without incurring a great expense. When the entire slope blooms, it is a sight to behold.

Amongst the more creative and specialized forms of gardening is container or trough gardening, which is attracting increased interest. Although basically employed by rock garden enthusiasts, it is a form of gardening which that can be accommodated by all, even on outdoor terraces, balconies or other limited planting spaces. The interest commenced in England about 50 years ago when the old-fashioned kitchen sinks, which were constructed of stone and which had been hollowed for various uses around farms and cottages were being replaced by more modern, manufactured appliances. They were mainly utilized as wash basins, kitchen sinks and animal feeding troughs. Typically, they were made of sandstone or limestone (easily worked). This soft stone is abundant in rural areas near quarries. Today, these old troughs, in various sizes and shapes are in great demand and command premium prices for trough gardening.

Given the limited availability of these stone troughs, substitutes have been devised. They are usually molded in wooden or cardboard frames to make the bed and the foundation walls. Various mixtures of cement, sand, peat moss, vermiculite or perlite are mixed and poured into the form to make the trough. The actual size and shape of these artificial troughs depends largely on the gardener's need, patience and creative commitment. Some nurseries, specializing in rock plants offer these troughs filled with diminutive species in scale with the containers. Of course they often include the tiniest hostas. Such

troughs are displayed either on raised walls or upon a raised stone or other upright base which not only permits excellent draining, but makes it easier to enjoy and work with the plants.

But there are alternatives to these cement base containers. Durable wood, preferably of cypress (*Taxodium distichum*) or redwood, treated with wood preservatives not harmful to live plants work well. Similar containers have also been utilized as window or ledge gardens for growing tiny plants. No matter what you start with, whether it be an old, stone kitchen sink, an old bathtub, or a Styrofoam or plastic tub, it is imperative to pierce a number or drainage holes into the base of the container irrespective of size or material. It is important to note that while these trough gardens may be left out of doors in England's mild winter regions, they do require some protection from the extremes of winter, particularly the early freezes before the plants have had a chance to harden off in colder climates. Patience is rewarded in creating an ideal, jewel-like garden with a wide assortment of tiny plants. Certainly, the small hostas will earn the space they take.

Let me conclude with the list of small hostas which are available and certainly worth trying out: (Numbers in ( ) are number of plants required/square yard and number required/square meter)

H. **'Amy Aden'** (Aden)—Variegated, very neat, white base with green and yellow stripes; green margins; flower scape in scale with mound; shade to ¾ sun; (49) (59)

H. **'Blue Moon'** (Smith)—Very blue; neat; smallest *tardiana*; good substance; floriferous; extra choice; shade to ¾ sun; (49) (59)

H. 'Blue Moon'

H. 'Chartreuse Wiggles', used on slope, have an animal-like aspect. Asarum in the background.

H. **'Celebration'** (Aden)—Variegated; neat; cream base with green margin; tends to be upright; very popular; shade to ¾ sun; (36) (43)

H. **'Chartreuse Wiggles'** (Aden)—Chartreuse to gold; very neat and unique; lance-shaped leaves heavily ruffled; rapid grower; small hosta award; shade to ¾ sun; (18) (22)

H. **'Excitation'** (Aden)—Chartreuse to gold; very neat; unique, ruffled leaves, sport of *H.* 'Citation'; shade to ¾ sun; (18) (22)

H. **'Geisha'** (Japan)—Variegated; chartreuse to yellow base with green margin; glossy leaves grow in unique, upright, twisting pattern; shade to full sun; (36) (43)

H. **'Little Aurora'** (Aden)—Gold; puckered; smallest *tokudama;* rapid grower; ¼ to ¾ sun; (12) (14)

H. **'Neat Splash'** (Aden)—Variegated; green, lance-shaped leaves with irregular cream stripes; rapid grower; stoloniferous; effective on slopes; shade to ¾ sun; (12) (14)

H. **'Pixie Power'** (Aden)—Variegated; cream-white base with green margin; neat; tiny jewel; shade to ½ sun; (49) 59)

H. **'Rock Master'** (Japan)—Tiny, frosted green which thrives in wide range of conditions; neat; shade to ¾ sun; (49) (59)

H. 'Geisha'

H. 'Little Aurora'

H. 'Sea Sprite'

H. 'Vanilla Cream'

H. 'Sea Sprite' (Seaver)—Variegated; yellow to cream base with wavy, green margin; rapid grower; stoloniferous; shade to ¾ sun; (18) (22)

H. 'Shining Tot' (Japan)—Tiny *venusta* with sun-proof, high-lustre, deep green, attractive foliage; neat; flower scape in scale with mound; very vigorous; shade to full sun; (56) (67)

H. 'Squiggles' (Aden)—Variegated; unique pinwheel; cream base with irregular green margin; shade to ¾ sun; (36) (43)

H. *tardiflora* (Japan)—Lustrous, dark green, lance-like leaves with red petioles; flowers heavily in fall; species "must"; shade to full sun; (16) (19)

H. 'Thumb Nail' (Epstein)—One of the smallest hostas ever propagated; tiny *venusta* with frosted green; very vigorous, good for reducing soil erosion; shade to ¾ sun; (56) (67)

H. 'Vanilla Cream' (Aden)—Chartreuse to gold to cream; very neat; heavy substance; unique; pest resistant; tends to grow flat; ½ to full sun; (36) (43)

H. *venusta* 'Variegated' (Japan)—Variegated; cream base with two-tone, green margins; vigorous in spite of small amount of chlorophyll; very attractive as a pot plat; very effective in brightening dark areas; shade to ¾ sun; (36) (43)

H. 'Thumb Nail'

Small Hostas in Difficult Places

VIII

DR. LILLIAN EICHELBERGER CANNON

A Woodland Setting for Hostas

A 26 acre home plot was found in Illinois about 35 years ago. It was called "The Timber" by the farmer who lived across the road. This was a true, virgin woodland, never farmed or used in any way. Mature, towering trees were everywhere in a glory seldom seen on the average home plot, or even in public parks. Towering White and Red Oaks, wide-girthed Black and Sugar Maples, majestic Black Walnuts that a furniture maker would give his eye teeth for, an assortment of ash, sycamore, Ironwood, apple trees, Sour Hickory, linden, elm, Siberian crabs, Red Bud all found a niche here. The place looked like the site for a botany class field trip. No builder had yet scraped off the soil, the soft, crunchy soil with untold tons of leaf mold. Underneath, the dormant wild flowers lay. It took a few years to realize what we had, these woods preserved for someone's gardening pleasure in the midst of surrounding farms.

The next spring, we saw wild flowers. Toothwort and Spring Beauties growing in masses by the thousands and opening before the Mertensias could bring the sky down to earth. The parade continued with Hepaticas growing in huge clumps of white, rose or lavender followed by the unfurling of the leaves and waxy flowers of Blood Root. How I wished that I knew more about time-lapse photography. Each day, I looked forward to a new spectacle. There were masses of Rue Anemone covering the ground like an early snow fall with their bloom. Patches of Trillium in bloom told us that spring had truly arrived while the ground became blue and purple with violets. The

surprise and wonder at seeing the unique Jack-in-the-Pulpits standing under their purple striped hoods. But all was not perfect in paradise, these spring flowers vanished soon after they had flowered to take their rest until the next spring. Voids were quickly filled by weeds in wide assortment. There were only two of us—and only available to garden on weekends, when the weather was suitable. The climate was cold, severly cold in the winter. The shade was dense in most areas. The soil was very acid, woodland soil, and then there was the problem of not disturbing the dormant wild flowers. Not least, there were 26 acres.

After much reading and talking to other gardeners with similar sites, we decided to try hosta. Something had to fill the voids left by the vanishing wild flowers. Something had to take up the space and light that would encourage weed growth. The woodland contains the main requirements for the growing of hostas, ideal soil and good shade. In fact, the soil is a sandy loam over gravel (good drainage) with a combination of mineral matter; clay and lots of decayed vegetable matter and leaf mold. The soil felt spongy—with great air spaces, and equally important, water-holding power. With plenty of water for foliage plants like hosta, even drought was no problem. The soil microorganism population was very high, an important factor in making potential soil plant foods available to plant roots. The sites where we planned to put hostas did have some light, sometimes dappled, sometimes fleeting, but typically

A woodland scene. from lower left (clockwise): Primula, Asarum, Bergenia, Pulmonaria, Heuchera, Uvularia, Arisaema, Liriope, Epimedium, Aruncus interspersed with hostas.

penetrating for a few hours, leaving shade most of the day.

Learning about the various species and cultivars of hosta was more exciting that we had expected. Even then, the variation in size, form, colors and potential use was more than we could digest in a short time. We knew that this was going to be a long-term project and that we would learn much along the way. Our first division of hosta came from a mail-order hosta specialist (sounds like a branch of medicine). These people were not only knowledge-able, they would guarantee that the variety chosen would be the one that you received. The hosta catalogs at the time could, in most cases, hardly be called catalogs. Very few had any kind of picture and anything approaching a description, much less an adequate description. In spite of "buying pigs in a poke," we have not been disappointed. The plants spoke for themselves.

Divisions are planted in the following way. Pick a special place under the trees where the wild flowers have vanished. In good soil, a trowel is sufficient to dig an ample hole for a division. Press the division against the side of the hole after cutting about ⅓ of the roots off, spread the roots out and cover with the removed soil. Use the handle of the trowel to poke soil between and around the roots as soil is added and then water gently for about 3 minutes. Plant single divisions about 1–3 ft. apart, depending upon their mature size. Plant in colonies, masses of 3, 5, or more to make an impact in a few years. While early spring is the best time for planting—almost any time seems to work with the possible exception of those received from warmer climes, which have not had a chance to "harden off" and you are approaching your early frost dates. Even in this case, if the planted hosta are slightly mulched, you are unlikely to have a problem. Do not apply a heavy mulch on freshly planted hostas until the ground is frozen. This will help prevent damage from burrowing animals (like mice). In general, established hostas do very well without mulching. In fact, they may do better, espe-cially in decent soil, when the harboring of the various creatures in the mulch is considered.

Your young hosta plants will increase in size—almost on a daily basis. The longer they remain in one site, the more beautiful in size, form and color. During the third spring, you can remove some divisions by slicing through the crown with a knife along lines that the divisions normally break and use a narrow shovel to lift out division slices (like pieces of pie) for transplanting at new sites. Be sure to replace the void with good soil. The major part of the clump has not been disturbed. Your neighbors may wonder where you got the new plants from. Eventually, your original divisions may seem to be crowded. This is a blessing. No room or light for weeds.

If you have need for plants in other areas, move some of the in-between clumps. Any hosta clump can be moved at almost any time. There is no such thing as an irreversible mistake in a hosta garden. The best time to move clumps is when the soil has some moisture, so that the soil will cling to the roots while the plant is being moved. Also, time your moves towards the onset of twilight if possible. If the clump is too big and your back is too small, move one-half a clump at a time. Match the soil level at the new site with the original soil level. Watering gently for about 3 minutes to settle soil around roots is sufficient. It is not necessary to tamp down. In fact, tamping down on wet soil tends to compact the soil structure. You're better off giving spaced 3 minute gentle waterings than puddling. The air spaces in the soil are worth something. Moving hosta clumps can be very creative—in probing to achieve a better color, form or textural balance.

At no time were any of our hostas cultivated as cultivation would destroy the dormant wild flower roots. More importantly, the hostas tended to eliminate the main reasons for cultivation. Consider reasons for cultivation: (1) to keep down weeds; (2) to keep soil open so that water and nutrition can penetrate for the absorption of food and moisture by the roots; (3) to break up soil so that organic particles may more easily be converted into new sources of food. Well, the hosta foliage removed conditions favorable to weed growth, and reduced water evaporation, thus keeping the soil cooler and more fit for soil microorganisms. No cultivation was needed. The covering of the wild flowers by the hostas during the summer months seems to aid rather than harm them. They seem to enjoy the cooler soil and the coverage which the hosta foliage provides.

It is not of course possible to lay down hard and fast rules for planting a hosta garden in a woodland. It has to be an act of creation that requires some patience. A woodland garden is an individual thing reflecting the tastes and requirements of the gardener. So much depends upon the kind and density of the trees. The removal of many of the lower limbs of trees (high canopy) has a dramatic impact on the quality of light and heat, as well as the success of your plants. While there must be cooperation between the gardener and nature, the range of adaptability of hostas goes a long way in insuring success.

The basic color in nature is green. It is a relaxing color, a cool color which serves as a background for the rest of flower color and it is the color that makes woodlands so restful and refreshing. Hostas easily add to that green with brocades, while their variations of green add interest and give shape to the entire landscape. Yet, even green can be dull. Touches of yellow or white in the garden not only contrast with green, they magnify each other's beauty. Hostas can also furnish the yellows and the whites while still allowing an element of continuity with the green hostas.

Our first hosta choices (1968) were species such as *H. tardiflora, H. sieboldiana* 'Elegans', *H. decorata, H. crispula, H. fortunei* 'Aureo-marginata' and *H. undulata.* There were not too many found in the market place in those years. As more gardeners became acquainted with hostas and their popularily increased, the nurseries (mostly mail-order) started to offer more species as well as some newer cultivars. Today, the species are typically passed over in favor of the new cultivars—and with good reason. Undoubtedly, the improved range of sizes, forms and colors in the new cultivars has had a lot to do with this shift. Each member of this remarkable genus has a personality. This personality becomes apparent as each somes into leaf. Some are thick, others thin. Some leaves are shaped as lances, others are shaped like ovals or hearts. Interestingly, the personality as well as the characteristics change as the plant matures. Some are different shades of green, or blue, or gold, or variegated with white or yellow either on the margins, or in the center. Some are large, others are medium, and still others are small, but each with its own individual shape, arrangement and venation. Some are fast growing, others slow and deliberate. All want good food and water, but do not want to be pampered and prefer not to be moved about. Being individuals, each type likes its own kind of place and if left to grow, will make mounds of foliage, which is more of a delight to the eye than their freely flowering heads (especially in the older cultivars). In most genera, we have been conditioned to first appreciate the beauty and diversity of the flowers. But hosta leaves demand most of the attention over a long period of time.

Hostas do not suffer from being alone. A single plant in a favorite spot or at a definite corner is a great way to enjoy its beauty and form. Allow it to grow to maturity and it will prove what it can do. A few of the

Woodland scene in which hostas dominate. (Garden of C. Lantis)

H. 'Gaiety', a bright spot in the shaded woodland.

newer hostas that I am now enjoying in the woods are: *H.* 'Fascination' (Aden), *H.* 'Flamboyant' (Aden), *H. fluctuans* 'Variegated' (Japan), *H.* 'Fragrant Bouquet' (Aden), *H.* 'Gaiety' (Aden), *H.* 'Gold Edger' (Aden), *H.* 'Janet' (Shugart), *H. montana* 'Aureomarginata' (Japan), *H.* 'Shade Fanfare' (Aden), *H. 'Sum and Substance'* (Aden), *H.* 'Summer Snow' (Cannon), *H.* 'Sun Power' (Aden) and *H. ventricosa* 'Aureo-marginata' (Bloom).

In these woods, there is no man-made watering system. Nature is relied upon entirely. Although there have been many droughts, the hostas never showed signs of suffering for want of moisture. There are many hard maples in these woods. Most gardeners think that the surface roots of hard maples prevent the luxurious growth of any plants under their branches. Our hostas grow well there because there is plenty of cool deep soil with plenty of leaf mold. The same is true under the tall Black Walnut trees. Hosta foliage covers the shaded floor from the bole to the outer branches of the trees.

The month of October provides sunny days with piercingly clear blue skies from sunrise to sunset. The air is heady and sparkling. Light frosts or light freezes at night may occur. The hostas begin to fade turning a bright yellow or a decorative gold. Most of the green and variegated plants begin to glow. The color change begins about the first week in October (in Illinois) and reaches its height in the third or fourth week. The

A Woodland Setting for Hostas

thicker the texture of the leaf, the denser the color. Their radiance and form resemble metal and are quite attractive. At the height of the color change, the mid-portion of some of the leaves remains green, forming an unusual contrast. There is no noticeable drying of the leaves. They are quite suitable for flower arrangements at this time. This last act in a long season is played against a background of other plants of other genera which seem to have given up.

Today, there are hosta beds through the woodland. The view is a splendid reward for the hard work of keeping a woodland. Hostas are good companion plants. They like to feel their neighbors pressing on every side and thread their roots among those of others for food and water. Leave the planting to grow larger and larger as the years go by. No cultivation. No coddling. Even the replenishing of the leaf mold is not thought about because nature takes care of that chore by way of the fallen leaves from the trees above.

A hosta enthusiast is never satisfied until someone else has been persuaded to do likewise. There are woodlands filled with trees and wild flowers waiting to be appreciated. Hostas can be invited to join the wild flowers. Here each season has its own beauty and each day its own experience. No one seeing a single hosta plant can have any idea of the beauty in masses of them. The possibilities of a hosta garden in a woodland are infinite. Each year will bring continued rewards and the promise of future development.

Late, fall coloring of *H. fluctuans* 'Variegated'.

IX

PAUL ADEN

Competitors in the Garden

With the multitude of real or imagined human problems, why be concerned about garden parasites? After all, they are outside of the house. What principles or enduring values are being threatened? Well, if I had to come up with 5 arguments, they might be: (1) "They" share without working, a good place to start. (2) "They" are too prolific. 2 or 3 aphids don't eat too much, or do too much damage. It's their relatives, invited ones as well as those produced by the original 2 or 3 in just a few weeks, which cause a real change in the neighborhood. (3) "They" are just too sneaky, hiding underneath leaves, in folded leaves, in crevices, or the shade of a small rock, all the places where you are apt not to look. With the high price of microscopes, your don't get a chance to see many of them in all their glory, and the thought that your ordinary senses aren't good enough is deflating. (4) "They" don't stay to themselves. Mingling with lots of beneficial creatures nearby, "they" are difficult targets. (5) "They" are not reasonable, not a single concern about our feelings when they "dispatch" our very choicest plants, leaving the weeds untouched.

Pests have been in gardens for a very long time, maybe before we humans took title, and from the way they act, they give one the feeling that we are infringing on their "turf." A final solution seems no nearer today, even after thousands of scientific papers on the subject. In fact, the situation may be getting worse. Those powerful, broad-spectrum (i.e., systemics), killing chemicals seem to create as many problems as they solve. After you've killed off all the susceptible pests, it's what's left that is worrying. The survivors, in too many cases seem to be laughing at our modern chemical efforts. The growth in pesticide-resistant pests seems to be outpacing our ability to develop new pesticides. After repeated sprayings, the pesticide won't work. In the meantime, you also are destroying the beneficial creatures, like praying manti, ladybugs, helpful wasps and beetles as well as a wide assortment of other useful organisms that are caught in the crossfire. If anything has changed, it is probably our acceptance of and dependence on chemicals in attempting to control our pests.

It wasn't too long ago, that if you bit into an apple and a larvae appeared to take a look, you simply cut away his lodgings and ate the rest. Not today, a fruit or vegetable, about to be taken into the mouth on its way to a bath of acid in the stomach, is unacceptable if it contains even a small intruder, no matter how magnificient his design. But requiring "perfection" in an apple has a price and the same is true in expecting a perfect garden. There is some comfort in just looking at your choice plants at some distance, and the chances are that you will not notice imperfections caused by some pest. At a distance, you may not know that you do not know. Anyway, gardens by their very scale lend themselves to a macro rather than a micro approach.

Elaborate spray programs and the industries that support them have a strong rationale, perhaps tied to our need for stability, control and predictability. It's the fine print on the pesticide packages (often ignored), and the knowledge that the fine print doesn't reveal that is disturbing. The display of pesticides, often on open shelves, much like a row of breakfast cereal, is disturbing. Reading is one thing, assessing its import is another. Invariably, the language of the fine print seems to relieve the manufacturer of much of his responsibility in your use of his product.

The U.S. Environmental Protection Agency is currently reviewing a number of the chemicals used primarily in agriculture, but available in many states to home gardeners. The chemicals suspected of causing cancer, or acute toxicity, or birth defects, or fetal deaths include (using trade names) Lasso, Temik, Amitrol, Kromad, Folcit, Captan, Bladex, Alar, Kelthane, Karathane, Lorox, Penta, TPTH and TCP. It is worth adding that these products are manufactured by major U. S. manufacturers, and any ban on their future use may not apply in other countries. Our living tissue may not be that different from that of pests. Similar building blocks are involved. The fact that many pesticides can pass from lung to blood or through skin to blood and that many users do not wear proper protective garb doesn't help. To assume that we are immune because we are handling the equipment is unreal. In too many cases, the lack of concern for wearing proper shoes, protective clothing or even a breeze that blows the spray back into the sprayer's face is hard to understand. The story of a little arsenic each day in the soup that finally gets its man is similar to many pesticides. A history of a series of small dosages, sometimes stored in the liver or fat, each too small in itself to do the job properly, has not been studied in all of its ramifications to our health twenty or more years later. The fact that a "smoking gun" relationship with the increase in cancer is not clear is not tantamount to a clean bill of health. Fortunately, there are alternatives to regular sprayschedules.

The concept that "NATURE KNOWS BEST" can easily lead to "ANYTHING GOES." The early cowboy movies used to distinguish the villians from the heros by the color of their hats. The attitude that allows the creatures in "black hats" to build up their populations at your plants' expense seems OK if you expect the creatures in "white hats" to eventually control them. At least that's the way the movie script always went. This faith in the power of goodness usually results in simplistic answers or expectations. So, lots of praying mantis egg cases are sold, as well as ladybugs. The quest for simple answers goes on. The

A pleasant garden, a likely source of food for some pests.

premise is that benefactors like the manti, when not praying, are adept at seizing and swallowing just the harmful pests in all sizes throughout the growing season. The stories perpetuated by birdlovers in extolling the virtues of birds as pest-controllers seem inflated. The premise is that if you feed the birds with birdseed of a suitable type; provide them with plants that offer fruit and berries; water in the form of fountains, birdbaths or ponds; and birdhouses or other safe havens for them to build a nest, thus keeping them nearby, they will then repay your kindness by feeding on all of the harmful pests of any stripe, size or flavor. Keeping the birds happy is certainly a worthwhile objective. It's just too bad that most birds are so fussy about what they eat. Like most other human problems, myth competes too often with reality.

Vigilance helps. Without making it a chore, the habit of noticing little irregularities has value. Poking behind leaves, or down into stalks, looking for the unexpected or anything disfigured, stunted, off-color, pitted, chewed or mottled, if nothing else, is a change of pace in the garden. Taking the offensive is the state of play here. Detect "them" while they are few in number. Then, a simple spot spraying or swabbing with a weak soap or rubbing alcohol solution works easily. Nip the few before procreation becomes a serious matter. Keep the job from growing. Well-timed, spot sprays match the solution to the problem.

Sooner or later, gardeners will learn that the recipe for successful growing of a plant is to simulate "natural" conditions in a garden. Remove the "right" materials or conditions (their needs) and the plant suffers. The same is true of pests. They can be cut down to size if their needs are understood. Consider controlling pests, not by using lethal chemicals, but by removing a material or condition that they need to thrive. Just as a small spotlight on a dark stage can cast a big shadow, there are times when a small expenditure of energy on our part results in a large impact on pests. It's like pulling weeds early. For example, destroying egg masses of slugs or safe havens with a good spring cleanup of leaves and debris keeps the initial startup population low.

In the battle for survival, not all plants are equal. So far, we have painted the plant as the passive target, waiting for a pest. Not so—most plant species are equipped to fight off pests. Some, but not all have exotic mechanical, physical or chemical devices to thwart pests. If you expose a petri dish loaded with bacteria to a bacteriostatic, like penicillin, you might find individuals or groups that almost seem to enjoy the drug. It is also true that some plant genera and individual species and their cultivars are better at

fighting pests off, or whose nature is such that pests have little interest in becoming acquainted. Some 10,000 compounds produced by plants in defense against insects and fungi have been identified, and many more are likely to exist. It should be noted that many of the compounds are execretion products, safely stored in plant cell vacuoles. If you choose your plants wisely, the odds of having pest trouble will be diminished.

By way of example, H. 'Sum and Substance' is a large, chartreuse to yellow cultivar with a thick, waxy, dense substance. Slugs have been placed on and near the plant, but left for areas of easier chewing. It is certain that a good part of the slug problem will be resolved by plant breeding. It is also worth mentioning that just as we humans are more likely to "catch cold" when we are "run down," keeping plants in vigor is a cost-effective way of avoiding or minimizing pest problems. The fact is that most hosta species and cultivars sustain only minimal, if any pest damage.

H. 'Sum and Substance' in late September. Note that there is no pest damage.

Slugs Slugs are not my favorite creature. Many people feel that "they" are the leading hosta pest. You can step into your garden on any moist, warm evening, flashlight in hand, and find these mollusks, up to 4 in. (10 cm) in length (land snails—they have only a vestige of their shell embedded in their back). Their color varies from tan to reddish brown to black, but they are still slugs. The mucous they exude surely leads to a visceral hesitation in picking them up. Under the right conditions, they are successful competitors in the garden. They eat well, breed well and keep good hours being in the garden when we, or other predators are not around. A small tongue, designed like a chain saw (radula) chips away parts of leaves with greatest ease—often leaving only a network of veins. They prefer the younger, softer, easier-to-chew tissues with less chlorophyll, less wax,

Slug at close range. Imagine difficulty in detecting these mollusks, if viewed in poor light, at a distance with an earth background.

Moisture is required by slugs, wherever it can be found during a drought. Shown is a slug emerging, after an evening in a watering can during a drought.

less density. In the morning, the holes in the leaves as well as the mucous trails on the ground clearly identify the night visitors.

The following observations are made with a full understanding of the risk undertaken by the author. Slugs are real competitors. The absence of a shell means that they have less need for calcium carbonate (lime as a building block) and can more easily fit into tight places. These creatures not only can swim in water, they can make their own road (mucous) on land. Any creature that can pass over the sharp edge of razor blades with grace is worth at least a second look. Like earthworms, they are hermaphroditic. They have male and female organs, but with a few exceptions, require 2 individuals for successful fertilization. That, however, is not their weak spot. Their egg masses of 25 or more are light-tan or brown, somewhat translucent ⅛ in. (1/20 cm) spheres. The eggs are something to behold in the light, which is where they usually will not be. Starting in late fall or early spring, look in an old flower pot, under debris or leaves, or in the middle of the remains of plant clumps. Some favorite clumps include Fern, Liriope, Bergenia, Heuchera, Cyclamen, Primula and Asarum. Once, I experimented with three lines of Liriope. The buildup in slugs was tremendous. Relief came when the project was disbanded and the line of Liriope was reduced to one. While in the egg or dormant stage, a little effort goes a long way. Scraping the eggs or slugs into a water jar with a few drops of dish washing detergent destroys

the eggs, as well as the adults. A good (March) spring cleanup will give you a low startup population in May.

If only the image of slugs could be changed, a deficit could be converted into an asset. The name would have to go. I wonder what the man who marketed pet rocks could do. Pet slugs? Slug races? Slugs climbing greasy poles? If only slugs could read and cooperate. A sign, "Reserved for Slugs," could help us get rid of some of our lesser plants. It is said that frogs, skunks and garter snakes will swallow slugs. Not a word, however, has been said about digesting them or about their excellent flavor. I have listened to the recital of several recipes for preparing slug dishes on three different continents. There was talk of boiling, of frying, of chopping, of butter, of soy sauce, of special vinegars, of marinating for months—and yet the results were always the same, they taste like rubber bands. Too bad. All that protein going to waste.

Slugs originated from creatures of the sea. They continue to breathe through their skin. That skin has to be moist, just as the membranes in our own lungs have to be moist for the easy transfer of gases. During a recent period of prolonged drought, there were almost no slugs about, except for a few that I found in the bottom of a watering can, slobbering about in the few drops of water left from the previous day's use. Slug skin is also easily damaged by ultraviolet light, so, putting those two factors together, you understand why the slug is a nocturnal animal. It has to find

Exhausted slug, after laying a fresh batch of eggs in late October. Eggs and slug were found in an old, empty flower pot.

a moist hiding place away from the light during the day, particularly days when the sun is with us.

Other than moving, gardeners have discovered ways of dealing with slugs, such as: (1) Avoid watering your garden in late afternoon or evening. Give the plants and the ground a chance to dry somewhat before the onset of evening. (2) Remove some of the undergrowth, some of the mulch. Remove some lower tree limbs to get some air moving. VENTILATE the garden and you will cut down on fungus as well as slug problems. (3) You could try to make the earth somewhat scratchy by sprinkling the diatomaceous earth used as filters in swimming pools. The idea sounds logical, although it makes a bit of a mess, but does it work? (4) You could try trapping them by providing "hiding places" such as shingles, half grapefruits, half melons, all of which create and "eyesore in their own right." Add that someone has to dump the creatures into a jar containing weak detergent solution each morning. (5) You could try old jelly jars or plastic covers placed at dusk at ground level with the last dregs of beer from dinner. Slugs like beer, or malt plus yeast or sugar water with some brewer's yeast. It could be the alcohol. Polls on the beer brand preferences of slugs have not been released. It is not certain whether they drown in the beer, or are too paralyzed to hide the following day. Again, someone has to dump the creatures each morning.

Chemical treatments, particularly at an early stage when the foliage is just starting to emerge from the ground seem to work well. While carbamate pellets and granules are effective, they are too toxic in humans and pets for my taste. Greenhouse-supply companies sell 7½% metaldehyde in pellets or large granules. One good source is: Orchid House, 1699 Sage Avenue, Los Osos, California 93402. I have used this compound and found it to be effective and safe. Place it in small mounds on the ground, protected somewhat from rain by overhead foliage near your choice plants about 6–10 ft. (2–3 m) apart as dusk approaches. It will attract slugs from 20 ft. (6 m) away. If you do not get too much rain, or you use gadgets that look like small umbrellas over the bait, it will last for at least 2 weeks. The dead slugs will be taken care of by the insects in a few days.

Root Weevils Occasionally, damage will be seen from the root weevils (Ex.—Taxus Weevil). Half-moon notches in the leaf margin are a sign. Weevils will likely be found near yews, rhododendron, holly and similar plants. The damage is usually minor and does not warrant a serious control program. You could either move the hosta clump, or try drenching the soil every month starting in May with malathion or a similar contact poison. Systemic pesticides also work. Since the most damage is done by larvae in the soil that can easily hide in the crevices of roots, it is almost impossible to eradicate them. The adult beetles, operating at night, are eaten by other beetles, parasitic wasps and flies, toads and garter snakes.

Mice Mulch applied in the fall or heavy leaf-fall before the ground is truly frozen can create a problem. It may encourage mice to take up residence. They will then burrow to seek hosta rhizomes, when there is little else to eat. The use of mulch as a labor-saving device may have been oversold to gardeners. Left out of the equation are the many pests that a mulch may harbor and concentrate near our plants. With the possible exception of setting small plants, in late fall, particularly in the northern climes, mulching is not necessary for the winter survival of "hardened off" hostas.

Deer Deer have been known to eat hostas, particularly in late fall or when other sources of food are scarce. I don't know if this says something about their sense of taste, or their sense of hunger. They eat the foliage of some hostas, but not others and the plant usually returns the following year. The typical, commercially available electrified garden fences cannot be counted on to work. Experiments with 8 ft. (2.2 m) deer fences set at a 60° angle to the ground have proved successful. The ends of some posts rest on the ground, giving the fence a certain amount of bounce. The fence is strung with number 18 wire (usually aluminum) in strands about 1 ft. (.3 m) apart. This type of fence has both height and depth.

Apparently, the deer has a problem leaping some height while also negotiating the depth. The deer seem to become confused and gives up. Write to N.Y. State Department of Agriculture, Agriculture & Markets, Division of Plant Industry-ADC, Building 8, State Campus, Albany, N.Y. 12235 for their booklet, *Deer Damage Control.*

Nematodes. In some parts of Japan (Southern Honshu), there is a problem with root nematodes. The nematodes cause root swellings as they feed on the roots. The conscientious Japanese nurseries with this problem grow their plants in pots of sterile soil, which are set on heavy # 9 wire fencing fixed at least 4 in. (10 cm) above the ground level. For plants already infected with nematodes, place the plant roots in water about 44–45°C (115°F) for 30 minutes. Repeat the treatment in 10 days. No known nematode problem obtains in the United States or England, possibly due to "predator" soil fungi, protozoa, other nematodes, microarthropods and possibly viruses.

Hostas, grown in sterile soil mix, atop metal mesh to prevent nematode infection in Japan.

Root swelling indicating nematode penetration.

Rot Problems with rot in hostas are relatively rare. Growth stops as leaf discoloring occurs. Leaves separate easily from crown, often with a noticeable odor. It is most likely to occur if division propagation is done in the hot weather of late summer the the cuts are rather crude. The plant at this time of year may not possess its usual vigor and ability to fight off bacterial infection, which typically occurs at wound sites below ground level. Dusting the wounds with sulfur or a fungicide (like benlate or benomyl) after removing all "soft" parts and allowing to air dry on a screen for about an hour helps. In general, over-watering plants resulting in a subsequent decrease in soil air is an important factor—another reason to water prudently. One of the forms of bacteria involved in the rot is called *Corticium centrifugum.* Their natural enemy, a fungus called *Trichoderma,* is normally present in most soils, but if not present, can be cultivated in moist sawdust and then used to innoculate the soil where the bacteria are a problem.

The maggots of fungus gnats are a factor in spreading rot. This is more likely in soils very rich in organic matter. Bacteria reside in the stomachs of the maggots, thus the insect carries with it at all times a culture of bacteria that can be injected into a wound when the maggot chews on the wounded area. Apparently, the bacterial action softens the wound area and makes for easier-chewing and digestion by the maggot. The bacteria benefit from this arrangement by being able to survive the winter within the fungus gnat eggs laid near or on top of the wound areas. A weak solution of mercuric chloride, corrosive sublimate, or chlorox seems to be effective against both the maggots and the bacteria causing rot. A general flying-insect killer, such as electric bug zappers, may control the flying fungus gnats, and probably helps control the eventual larvae population, especially in indoor/greenhouse environments.

Virus Though quite rare in hostas, attacks are sometimes seen, typically in bizarre deformities such as very twisted and distorted foliage; discoloration, often a mottled or variegated appearance, not unlike that caused by a deficency of certain trace elements; or stunting often appears as a dwarf rosette in which stems fail to elongate; or ringspots, pale rings on the foliage. This is an extremely rare in hostas. The distortion typically disappears as subsequent growth occurs. One huge hosta clump in my garden, and only one, consistenly shows the influence of viral attack in early springs, on a few leaves, but doesn't appear on later-emerging leaves.

Viruses verge on the border between living and nonliving. Their structure is gene-like, too small to be seen with an optical microscope. When they penetrate the cells of a susceptible host, they somehow are able to reprogram the host's genes to work for the virus.

While viruses are frequently spread by tools used on infected leaves before working on susceptible, healthy leaves, I have seen no evidence of this in hostas. Insects like leafhoppers and aphids have been known to spread viruses in other genera, but I have never known of this transmission in hostas.

If a plant continues to display crazed, twisted or distorted, discolored, or mottled parts, destroy it by burning. It's better to play it safe. There are no sprays for viruses. A team of research workers of Washington University, in St. Louis, and the Monsanto Company have recently reported success in "vaccinating" plants against viral attack. Chances are that if a "crazy-looking" plant shows up in your hosta bed, you do not have the "unique" hosta of the century.

The other pests in the typical garden are of minor significance for hostas. The large numbers of pests which thrive on sun plants are not as common on shade plants, though they are of more concern in greenhouses or nursery growing beds. Included are spider mites in hot, dry, conditions which seem to attack a few species or cultivars, but do not bother the rest. Usually a forceful water spray, directed to the underside of leaves is sufficient to control them. Aphids can occur, but are again, fortunately, easily controlled by a forceful spray or a weak, soapy solution. The two generations of Inchworm (beetle larvae) do very minor damage that can be avoided by not planting under trees like White Oak, which harbor them.

The aim of this chapter has been to give the gardener a useful reference to all the pests which might concurrently attack hostas. But there is the danger that the "messenger," and more important, the genus, *Hosta* will be killed in the process. Let the hostas speak for themselves. With the exception of slugs, the vast majority of gardeners using hostas to solve garden problems will never experience or worry about most of the pests mentioned.

Leaf distortion caused by viral attack.

X

ANDRE VIETTE

Successful Companion Plant Combinations

Hostas contribute a wide variety of color, foliage types and stunning, bold textures in a range of sizes rivaled by few other plant genera in the landscape. Companion plants, including perennials, annuals and bulbs, complement the hosta planting by (1) effectively extending the season of garden interest, (2) providing a source of variety, in furnishing a wide range of complementary color, texture, shape and flower form.

Most of the companion plants discussed will prosper in bright shade, filtered shade or high shade, another way of saying that they need at least 4–6 hours of light. As deciduous trees are the main source of shade for the home garden, the tree canopy permits light to penetrate, especially in the early spring. As the emergence of hostas averages about 3 weeks after the last frost date, that gap in time is nicely filled by companion plants, especially the early spring flowers and bulbs. While it is still too cold to spend much time in the garden, the very early and active companion plants not only foretell of things to come in the new growing season, they can bring their most welcome and cheerful color after a dull winter. The early spring companion plants are not "true" companions, however, as they typically have little appeal after flowering, as maturing foliage builds energy for next year's flowers, and just as many of the early bloomers start to go dormant or pass their peak, the hostas and "true companions" are taking over, the fit is perfect, almost like the changing of the guard. Hostas serve particularly well in this situation, as they

perform until the frost, even without the presence of bloom.

Some "true companions," including flowering perennials, will tolerate deeper shade, even the dense shade of a thick evergreen forest or maples, but most prefer half shade or bright shade. A little judicious pruning, particularly of the lower limbs, can provide an environment which will benefit both the hosta and companion plants.

The companion herbaceous perennials add interest, particularly in a garden dominated by hostas. For example, hostas are quite restful to look at, especially when used as a groundcover, as the general view is one of overlapping horizontal planes. Rest has its place, but imagine all pets or all humans possessing but one shape, or even the same personality. Those companion plants that add zest to the garden are likely to exhibit variation in the form of a vertical line form here, a delicate fine foliage texture there, as examples, helping to complement the robust and impressive hosta.

There are some special problems in making blanket recommendations. Just as climatic conditions vary from region to region, so do conditions in different parts of a garden. Wind patterns, soil types, light exposure, the amount of protective snowfall, the steadiness or variability of temperature, cloudcover and precipitation patterns all play a part in setting a microclimate. Considering only the east coast of the United States, winters in Maine are easily −30°F (−35°C) with a heavy snowcover to Long Island

Companion, heraceous perennials add zest to the garden. Note the vertical, as well as the fine, texture elements in this scene.

where the temperatures dip to −10°F (−23°C), often without the benefit of snowcover to the milder winters of Georgia with little snow. A move 50 miles inland typically results in greater ranges between the year's high and low than experienced along the shore.

All of the mentioned complicating details, and more, urges discipline on my part, that the plants recommended in this chapter are hardy and will thrive over a wide range of conditions, based on my observations and evaluation over a period of many years. Low maintenance, as well as plants with an evergreen character for the winter garden have been given extra attention. In many cases, only one form is listed. This does not mean that it is the best species or cultivar, whatever that is, it simply means that the plant listed is a good one to start with. Invasive plants, no matter how beautiful, have been avoided.

The plants discussed in this chapter all possess considerable merit, in and of themselves. But, in addition, they add a measure of extra spice and variety when used with hostas. Not all of the plants described are easily available locally, for nurseries dealing in choice plants have never been restricted to a particu-

lar region. So, it may take some searching through catalogs to locate those best suiting your taste or situation. The plants all deserve the search and the opportunity to find a place in your garden, at least on a trial basis. The potential is there to enrich your garden experience. Number in first ( ) = number of plants required per square yard; Number in second ( ) = number of plants required per square meter at maturity.

Acorus gramineus **'Variegatus'** 6–12 in. (15–30 cm), evergreen grass, typically yellow and green or white and green; many named cultivars exist; does well even in full shade, soil must be more moisture-retentive with more sun; does well with small green, gold or blue hostas. (9) (11)

Anemone japonica, A. hupehensis 12–48 in. (30–120 cm); fall blooming, the charming windflowers have lovely cut-leaf foliage throughout the season which gives rise to exquisite flowers atop 1–4 ft. (30–120 cm) stems. Fall anemones tend to spread and should be given ample room; light shade. Mulch heavily for winter with oak leaves in colder climates, works well with gold and green hostas. (9) (11)

Acorus gramineus 'Variegatus' with Blue Squill in early spring.

Arisaema sikokianum

Arum italicum 'Pictum' with *H. fluctuans* 'Variegated'.

Arisaema sikokianum A most spectacular variegated Jack-in-the-Pulpit, 12–24 in. (30–60 cm), starts out looking like a carrot standing on its head in early spring; a new surprise almost every day. Leaf center is wide and irregularly silver, topped off by cluster of orange berries before it goes dormant in summer; needs rich soil with good drainage; lends itself to setting on a slope for easier observation.

    A. candidissimum 18 in. (45 cm); exquisite white flowers tinged rose in June. (4) (5)

Arum italicum 'Pictum' Arrowhead, marbleized leaves emerge in the fall and shine out through winter. Surprising, as it looks like a tropical plant to some. Great contrast with hosta foliage, particularly the golds and variegated hostas with some white. Flowers in June, look like chartreuse, hooded candles; forms dense orangebead lollipops on a stick during the summer and then goes dormant for 6 weeks; in rich, moist soil and light shade, it develops into a colony in a few years; works well with hostas with some white variegation, Ex. *H.* 'Resonance'; excellent addition to flower arrangements. (8) (10)

Asarum (Shuttleworthii) 'Callaway' This wild ginger, 4–6 in. (10–15 cm) in height, is used for its unusual, mottled, evergreen foliage. Leaves turn mahogany

The Hosta Book

green in winter; flowers in spring only spotted when leaves are pried apart to see base of stems. *Asarum European,* 4–6 in. (10–15 cm)—exhibits round, glossy, metallic-like green foliage and shape of leaves contrast well with yellows or greens of nearby hostas; gingers do extra well in rich, fibrous, woodland type soil; many Japanese variegated forms. (16) (19)

Astilbe chinensis 'Pumila' Long-flowering, lilac-rose trusses atop 12 in. (30 cm) scape during the summer; fern-like leaves; tolerates drier soil than most during the growing season; takes about ½ shade well; stoloniferous, will cover a square yard in 3–4 years; prefers light, sandy soil high in organic matter with adequate moisture. This charming plant has cut-leaf foliage which makes a distinctive contrast with the simple and bolder foliage of yellow hosta forms as well as those with some white in their variegation. Other cultivars range in height from 20–48 in. (50–120 cm). As a group, Astilbe do not tolerate drought conditions and must be watered during dry periods. (4) (5).

Athyrium nipponicum (Japanese Painted Fern); formerly called *A. goeringianum* 'Pictum', certainly one of the most specular of the hardy ferns; 24 in. (60 cm) fronds delicately blending grey-green with stems of wine-red combinations are typically

Athyrium nipponicum with *H.* 'Fragrant Bouquet'.

offered; grey, blue, various shades of green and red are becoming available in sizes from 8–40 in. (20–100 cm); best color in partial shade; color(s) may vary during the season; deciduous; prefers rich, moisture-retentive soils; best color in partial shade; requires watering during extended periods of drought; lacy, airy frond character offers a fascinating contrast with bold hosta foliage, especially the light greens and large-leafed blues. (4) (5)

Bergenia strachei 'Alba'

Molina caerulea 'Variegata' Variegated Purple Moor Grass; 16–24 in. (40–60 cm); neat, attractive yellow and green grass that prefers partial shade; requires good drainage; contrasts well with nearby small green, gold or blue hostas. (4) (5)

Ophiopogon planiscapus nigrescens Something really different in the garden; neat, symmetrical purple-black mounds about 4 in. (10 cm) have 6 in. (15 cm) spray of deep lavender flowers in the summer followed by black berries; evergreen, creeps slowly, needs moisture-retentive soil with good drainage; contrasts very well with nearby chartreuse or gold small hostas. (16) (19)

Platycodon grandiflorus Balloonflower 15–20 in. (37½–50 cm); adds captivating beauty to the garden with its alluring balloon-shaped buds (that kids love to 'pop') and wide, attractive blue, white or pink flowers from summer to fall; double forms exist. A great combination with the golden or light green hostas, Ex. *H.* 'Excitation', *H.* 'Invincible', partial shade. Mark site to avoid damage during early spring cleanup. (4) (5)

Polygonatum odoratum 'Variegatum' Japanese Solomon's Seal 24–36 in (60–90 cm); graceful, arching habit, somewhat vertical, with yellow-margined leaves offer interesting contrast to green or blue hostas nearby, pendant, fragrant, white flowers in late spring followed by blue-black berries, thrives even in full shade, excellent, yellow, fall color; colonizes in moist soil; good material for flower arrangements. (4) (5)

Polygonatum odoratum 'Variegatum', adding a change of form and interest in a hosta bed.

Shown in foreground is *Platycodon grandiflorus*, while hostas and hemerocallis fill the background. The dark blue of the platycodon flowers seem to recede, while the bright flower colors of the hemerocallis seem to advance, creating an illusion of closeness and crowding.

Pulmonaria saccharata 'Roy Davidson'

Primula sieboldii, P. japonica Gardeners should seek out the hardier garden forms; rosettes of lettuce-like leaves produce sprays of flowers in the spring that range from pink, magenta, blue, rose to white in late spring to early summer; contrasts well with nearby small chartreuse or gold hostas; require moisture-retentive soil with good drainage; *P. japonica* types tend to show flowers in candelabra displays. Beware of greenhouse forms that have entered the market and are not hardy out-of-doors. (9) (11)

Pulmonaria Lungwort Many forms exist, typically 8–12 in. (20–30 cm) mounds with succulent, rough-look, many forms blue tints speckled with white dots that have flowers very early in the spring that vary from blue to rose or white on 8–24 in. (20–60 cm) scapes; creeps slowly; partial shade with moisture-retentive soil with good drainage; contrasts beautifully with nearby yellow or blue hostas or hostas showing white variegation. (4) (5).

Saxifraga fortunei 'Rubrifolia' Bronze-red foliage (carmine beneath), that forms succulent-like clumps; wide sprays of white flowers in fall; requires cool soil, sheltered position; some mulch in northern winters; great contrast with chartreuse or gold hostas. *S.* ✕ *urbium* 'Aurea Punctata' London

Pride; richly variegated gold and green; looks like big Hens and Chicks; partial shade, good drainage; prodigious flower sprays of pale pink flowers on 9 in. (22½ cm) stems. (9) (11)

The yellow margin of *Tricyrtis hirta* 'Miyazaki' contrasts nicely with blue hosta seedling.

Tricyrtis hirta 'Miyazaki' Late summer to autumn flowers; light lavender heavily dotted with purple, 12–36 in. (30–90 cm); flowers nestled in leaf axils, hairy stems and leaves; prefers rich, moist, acid soil. (4) (5).

Shown from low right (clockwise): *Uvularia sessilifolia, Arisaema sikokianum, Disporum sessile* 'Variegated', *H.* 'Spritzer', *Heuchera americana.*

Uvularia grandiflora Bears pendulous yellow flowers on arching stems. This is a very hardy, long lived native plant with attractive bright green foliage—the best of the bellworts. Spring—12–18 in. (30–45 cm)—yellow flowers. (9) (11)

Yucca filamentosa (Variegated forms containing yellow, white or pink tints) Evergreen; surprisingly good companion plant to hostas in partial shade as long as soil has good drainage. Yellow variegated forms are very impressive adjacent to blue, bold hostas like *H.* 'Blue Umbrellas'. Quite useful as a foundation plant, furnishing a valuable vertical line. (1) (1)

A truly magnificent shade garden is created by selecting many diverse, outstanding plants. These companion plants bestow their own individual attributes upon the shade landscape while offering the balance of variation that maintains interest throughout the garden. Each in their own way, companion plants extend the range of color, form and texture throughout the season, as well as your pleasure in gardening.

Yucca filamentosa 'Color Guard', an evergreen, vertical accent that performs remarkably well in considerable shade.

XI

PAUL ADEN

Landscape Concepts

What is surprising, in light of the continuing thirst for individual identity, is that the landscape pattern of a lawn surrounded by a perimeter of a few evergreens, shrubs and annuals is so common and so uniform. One wonders if home landscapes are designed by committee. Thank God for House Numbers. The stories of people who couldn't read the numbers, so couldn't find the house (sometimes their own) have a basis in the rigid uniformity and conformity of most domestic landscapes.

Lawn grass, the most prevalent plant in most domestic gardens, demands almost continual sunlight, lots of air flow (almost invariably), so is not a likely candidate to succeed in the shade. The chances are that you now have larger grass areas in the shade that could be better utilized. Setting in a perennial bed may even help some people find your house.

The precise reasons why many people no longer take care of their own lawns may never be known, although I could come up with some educated guesses. It seems preferable today to have lawn-care trucks arrive every 10 days or so, their energetic crews proceeding to spray, fertilize, cut, edge and sweep according to a set routine. Even the bill is routine, and in complete accord with the calendar. Little is unexpected, or exciting. Such a routine is neither cheap, nor desirable, particularly in view of the fact that it keeps you from gardening, one of the oldest and most human of man's endeavors.

It is sad that most homeowners are unaware of what is involved in growing a good lawn. Yet, lawn grass, as measured by the percentage of space occupied, dominates the small, modern home setting. Moving pictures and magazine ads routinely picture absolutely magnificent, vast sweeps of lawn grass in England ... certainly impressive, status-building and expensive. It is instructive, that even though temperatures are moderate and rain is evenly distributed during the year in England, ideal conditions for grass, the lawns shown in the pictures are typically no longer in private ownership. They have largely been shifted to the public domain and supported by the general taxpayer. Growing lawn grass is not only expensive, it is not easy—ask the grounds

Vast sweeps of lawn at this estate are impressive.

A home landscape near the front entrance, filled with perennials, assures greater individual identity.

Lawn makes magnificent paths between plant beds.

crew of a golf course, or a ball park, or a homeowner committed to his lawn. Those pictures of horses running on a magnificent green grass in Kentucky, where the average topsoil typically is over 10 ft. (3 m) deep, are impressive. Let me tell you a trade secret, the "green" in lawn-seed and lawn-fertilizer ads is sometimes exaggerated by spraying with a bright green dye before pictures are taken. The odds are that your home site soil and climate are not even close to those in Kentucky or England. Very few places are.

Yet, grass does have a place in landscapes, it makes magnificent paths between plant beds and furnishes an esthetic setting for balance to flowers and foliage plantings. The key word is "balance." My brief is that while grass is a great leveler, its widespread overuse is boring and a landscaping cliche. The fact that grass is almost in the default position (automatic mode) when landscaping decisions are made, to the virtual exclusion of other options, indicates that the value of grass has assumed near mythic proportions and has been oversold. The vision of the vast sweep of lawn (historically useful in detecting potential intruders) on an English estate cannot be duplicated in the typical residential landscape, if only for reasons of scale. The myth that grass is much easier to maintain than other plants was true when hired gardeners were doing the work and labor was not only competent, but cheap.

The recent revival of interest in perennials undoubtedly reflects not only the recognition that a garden consisting primarily of grass is a burdensome thing, but that the sterile sameness of neighborhoods can be relieved, that a home can be distinguished by landscaping with perennials. The same line of thought can incidentally, also result in reduced

maintenance effort. Some perennials, like hostas, happily remain in one site for 30 or more years, barring the gardener's wish to divide or shift, for landscape reasons. This is another way of saying that perennial beds do not have to be replanted every year, no longer making it necessary to start each spring from ground zero, as is the case with annuals. The reason is simple enough, perennial plants do not rapidly drain the soil of its nutrient reserve, as do many annuals. They do not demand extra effort in replenishing nutrient reserves to maintain plant vigor and performance. Surprisingly, hostas become more beautiful and perform better (become more pest-resistant and sun-tolerant) with each passing year.

An indication of the toughness of hostas. Bare root clump was left upside down during an entire, open winter. Shown are new shoots growing down and then up through the root mass in early spring.

Perennials provide a number of interesting qualities, in addition to their flowers. Spacing visits to a perennial garden every two weeks will lead to new discoveries on every visit. Foliage perennials, like hostas, offer an extra bonus as the show is not over when the flowers are spent. The average period of bloom of most perennials is about three weeks. But hosta foliage is attractive as long as the mound is above ground, a substantial period of time when compared with the average perennial flowering period. Its foliage not only rivals the beauty of flowers, particularly that of variegated mounds, it can also set off different areas, or gardens within the garden. Many hostas seem to extend the day by "glowing" at twilight, and extend the fall season by foliage changes to exotic golds and greens. For the busy, suburban homeowner, foliage perennials, like hostas, help make the garden more manageable by leaving little room or light for weeds, while offering the special advantage of mid-summer flowering, a time when few other genera can make any offering to summer flower arrangements or corsages.

The knowledge, skill and strength required to create a pleasing, residential landscape is well within the average person's grasp and budget. Just as it took time for our ancestors to learn which plants are edible, learning about and developing skill in working with living plants takes time, albeit it is "quality" time. And you will find that the initial bewilderment and sense-of-being-overwhelmed-stage doesn't last very long. Small gardening successes go a long way in building confidence. Unfortunately, too many of us in the modern household do not have a relative who is actively gardening, to serve as a garden-mentor, someone who can give us a hand, especially at the beginning. Fortunately, gardening has always had a social and a community aspect. An organized, gardening group, whose members will gladly help another get started is never far away.

Teaching yourself does have some benefits. The results of "discovery" are not something to be taken lightly. Gardening is not just a form of exercise, it is a lifelong pursuit, a pursuit in which victories do occur and a sense of mystery is always close. The miracle of a seed or young plant developing to maturity still fills most people with wonderment. Dr. A. P. Saunders, a famous peony hybridizer, explained his activity and zest at age 95 by saying, "I've always got something to look forward to."

The author cannot guarantee that if you start gardening, you will live a "quality" life to at least the age of 95, but like chicken soup, at least it won't hurt. The level of activity in the garden can be tailored to fit, not only the time devoted to other activities, but also

A landscape experiment that is worth trying. Slopes of "valley" path are lined with tall, ornamental grasses and hostas that change considerably during the growing season.

A tree set in midlawn, ringed by a bed of *H.* 'Shade Fanfare', makes the garden more manageable. (Garden of Dr. J. Gauthier)

the constraints of your budget by spreading expenditures over a comfortable period of time. Indeed, you should give yourself the time to seek out those plants to create the kind of landscape that says something about you, something you can be proud of, and which satisfies your sense of beauty and the uses to which you put your garden. Don't settle for a neighbor's throwaway plants nor landscape ideas. The merry-go-round of being a perpetual beggar or beginner does not satisfy. It's not really a question of the cost of plants, but rather how much effort you must invest to realize the "right stuff" that is important. No investment, in money, time or energy, is worth much if you quickly tire of it, or it quickly tires of you. If the plants you purchase bring you satisfaction, earn the space you have given them, then the actual cost is low, especially when amortized over the years of satisfaction.

A brief discussion of the ramifications of gardening in the shade is in order. Many plants in nature are found in shade only at lower elevations, while those same plants thrive in strong sunlight at higher altitudes. If the shade-loving plant at sea level is the identical plant as the sun-loving plant on the mountain, what's the story? It gets a bit more complicated when you consider that while light influences temperature, it does so to a different degree at different sites. Take the temperature of plots of beach sand, loam and rich humus at the same time. At 2 PM, the sand is clearly hotter that the others. At 2 AM, the

sand is clearly cooler. Now, repeat the experiment with a set of identical plots on a mountain, where the air is thinner. The mountain temperatures are cooler than those found at sea level. It begins to look as if temperature is at least as important as light in a plant's success. Perhaps just as important, light influences not only the soil temperature, but also the ability of the soil to retain moisture, as evaporation increases with temperature. Now, add the type of creatures, seen or unseen, that live in the soil, many of which play a key role in a plant's survival. Lastly, add the availability of nutrients of each of the soil types, "Shade-loving" becomes an overly simple term.

In a recent, conversation with Beth Chatto, the English plantswoman, about developing successful stratagems in growing unusual plants, she said, "The ecology of the plant in the wild is all important. Try to create similar conditions in the garden, as the plant might find in the wild." This advice is pertinent, particularly to hostas found in extreme conditions,

The "right stuff" is worth seeking. Shown are *Rhododendron yakushimanum, Athyrium nipponicum* and hostas.

such as bogs or dry conditions. Few of us will ever have the opportunity to explore the ecology of our plants, but special treatment, when necessary, is described in other chapters, and this information is readily available, as it applies to other landscape plants in libraries of public arboreta.

We all know the changes in the quality of light within our homes during the different seasons, and at different times of day. In the spring and fall, light penetrates deeper into a particular room. In the winter, with little or no foliage to screen the light, a room can be alive with light, if only for a short time. Homes surrounded by deciduous trees, rather than evergreens, typically have lower winter heating bills. Light adds considerable interest in the same way to the shade garden. Different areas are either bathed or spotlighted with light at different times of day, at different seasons during the year. In many cases, the light seems to be doing a slow dance from spot to spot. It is no secret that the color and intensity of light varies with the season, the time of day, and the amount of leaf screening. These differences help to explain the large size of some plants found in deep shade at mid-summer.

Further, the quality of garden light can be changed, almost instantly. The recent gypsy moth infestation in our region made for an unusual mid-summer scene—save for the lack of snow, it looked like winter. Not a single leaf to be seen. Tornadoes and gales also have a way of thinning trees. A 200 year old White Oak did not bend enough during a tornado recently. Seeing this colossus keeled over like a dying, prehistoric, giant dinosaur, perched up somewhat on its lower limbs seemed to say something about the quest for eternity. The resulting light changes in the garden were dramatic—even disastrous. We have since started planting a few young trees, so that the garden will not continue to be overly dependent on a very few mature trees.

Getting more light into the garden is usually beneficial if the change in amount is moderate. Removing the lower limbs of some trees not only changes the light reaching the understory plants, but also changes the range of plants that can be grown, as well as increasing the general air flow. Thinning or "limbing up" certainly will make formerly dark, and perhaps dank areas a lot more pleasant, a welcome plus on hot summer days. It also will inhibit outbreaks of fungus diseases as well as pests which depend on continuous moisture, such as slugs.

The light-screening characteristics of various tree species also determines which species will grow well nearby. Most maples, and some beeches not only produce very dense shade, but their overzealous surface roots present problems as well. In general,

small domestic landscapes should not include giant, forest trees, even though they are sold in good size at a low price. In 15 years, it may cost a small fortune to remove the tree bargain. Messy trees, with a heavy fall of snapping branches, seed pods or large, inedible fruit and shallow roots, such as Willow, Silver Maple, Sweet Gum and Tulip, often end up being more trouble than they are worth. Seek out small trees that offer flowers, high pest and wind resistance, a haven, and perhaps food for birds as well as good fall color, such as small-fruited Crab Apple and Pear, Kousa Dogwood, and Japanese Maple. The smaller, home-size tree species which allow some light penetration provide not only far more garden interest, but conditions which are conducive to the growing of a wider range of plants and animals in the garden.

Turning now to practical matters, the site for plant beds must first be selected. From the gardener's viewpoint, SUCCESS means having plants which provide magnificent flowers and foliage over the longest possible period of time. To a high degree, the needs of plants and the gardener's desires are not far apart. It is almost inevitable that the garden will become shadier, as it ages. The aging of both garden and gardener is fortunate, time spent in the shade is not only more pleasant, it is more relaxing. True, there are fewer flowers in the shade garden, but they last longer with colors that hold up better. While fewer seeds are produced by plants in the shade, this is a matter of little importance, unless you are going to embark on a long-term breeding and evaluation program. True, fewer leaves are produced in the shade, but they are larger and sustain less damage from "sun pests." Just as important from the plant's point of view, the "big picture" is better in the shade, particularly for foliage plants like hostas, in that water losses from the soil are reduced.

A garden hose provides a perfect tool to experiment with bed shapes. Lay the hose on the ground in the general area of your planned perennial bed. Vary the outline made by the hose as you look at it from different vantage points. Imagine different "resting or looking points" in a walk through the garden. If possible, think in terms of making a good picture. Forget about relatively small circular beds, they will only lead you in circles. Try making the bed more than 6 ft. (2 m) wide to give you more options. Try utilizing changing levels (i.e., slopes), as different planes in a bed add interest, a stratagem than is particularly true with hostas, as the normal horizontal line of most hostas is converted into a dramatic "tiered" effect. Make a shape that is easy for the eye to follow, with no squared-off corners, no sharp angles, just gentle curves which lead your eye gently.

Design the shape so that as your eye moves along

Design the bed shapes so that there is a sense of mystery ahead.
Note the "framing" of the garden by small tree branches, helping to
create a "keyhole" effect.

it, there is a sense of mystery ahead, so a viewer is required to walk further into the property in order to see areas that were 'just beyond' the area in view at the outset of your walk. The larger hostas, with foliage easily seen at a distance, and placed at key "bend" points, but only partially seen, are quite effective in exciting curiosity. In other words, provide visitors with an incentive to walk through your future garden in order to see it by arousing curiosity, not a bad recipe to create interest. The shape of the bed is especially critical near the patio. Plan to have at least part of it facing south so that flowers leaning towards the sun can be seen by the observer. If the lines of the bed and the house are not quite parallel, but converge somewhat, so much the better as the feeling of depth is enhanced. Smaller hostas at the end of the view, while larger hostas are at the beginning also enhance

Shape beds around the patio area so that there is room for
screening plants.

the perception of depth. When the visitor reaches the point where he (she) can now see, what could not be seen before, and is surprised with a particularly beautiful hosta clump or bed, you have a landscape concept which I call AMBUSH, to be discussed later.

Identify an area where you would enjoy relaxing (the patio?), and so want some privacy. Shape the beds around this area so there is room for screening plants, which need not absolutely block out potential eyes to give a sense of privacy, relaxation and security. Many of the taller, background hostas serve effectively as screening plants, particularly when they are set in a raised bed around the relaxation area.

The thought of setting your plants in the bed without removing the grass should be instantly dismissed. The idea of cutting around perennial clumps with a mower, or removing grass that will wander into your clumps from all directions is not worth two nanoseconds. Some thoughts on removing grass include:

1. First off, mow the grass with your mower set at the lowest setting.

2. Spread a cheap, chemical fertilizer over the area (like granular 5-10-5), at double the recommended dosage for lawns, water the fertilizer in.

3. Place the backsaver sets of twelve sheets of newspaper, overlapped on top of the grass to be removed. If necessary, shape the newspaper with scissors to fit the contour of the new bed. Hold the paper down with soil or small rocks.

4. If you apply 1 in. (2.5 cm) of soil on top of the newspaper, wait 2+ months before planting. If you use about 6+ in. (15 cm) of soil, planting can be undertaken immediately. Patience pays off, since the grass will be reduced to a rich soil before the newpaper disintegrates. The process can be speeded up somewhat by watering frequently after the soil is set atop the newspaper. It also helps to mix ⅓rd part peat moss, leaf mold or mature compost into the soil applied before it is spread out.

5. Alternatively, spread 6 mil or thicker black plastic after the fertilizer and water has been applied instead of newspaper. Keep the plastic from blowing with some stones or bricks. Wait about 2+ months before removing the plastic and planting.

6. If you have planned a larger area, consider renting or hiring a rototiller of at least 8 horsepower. If the planned bed area tends to hold water after a heavy rain, spread 3 in. (7.5 cm) of coarse, builder's sand before rototilling. If the area, on the other hand, has trouble retaining moisture after a heavy rain, spread 3 in. (7.5 cm) of peat moss, leaf mold or compost before rototilling. If standard 6 cubic feet bales of peat moss are used, estimate the number of bales (6 cubic feet size) needed by multiplying the square feet

area to be covered by the depth, in inches, by .0153. If surface tree roots are a problem, a bit of chopping will help avoid breaking rototiller tines. Rototilling works best when the soil is reasonably dry. At least 2 passes from different directions will be required to do a good job. Don't be surprised if neighbors appear who you haven't seen in months. There will come a day when all signs of grass are gone. The bed shape is right, the soil looks and feels great. Now the real fun begins.

The AMBUSH concept of landscaping has already been mentioned. But, let us deal with the basic landscaping concepts in some kind of order so they are easier to remember. They are VARIETY, AMBUSH, REPETITION and INSPIRATION—four in all. V A R I is the acronym.

Plant variations in groupings should not be random. Shown, starting with hosta (clockwise): *H. fluctuans* 'Variegated', Hemerocallis, Acorus, *Carex* 'Bowles Golden Sedge', Asarum, Helleborus.

Hostas offer continuity in the garden. (C. Allen. Courtesy of Klehm Nursery)

Closeup of the variegation found in a mature leaf of *H.* 'Reversed'.

The art of gardening involves the placing of plants and their effect upon their neighbors. *H.* 'Shade Fanfare' near conifers and pink-flowering astilbes. (Garden of R. J. Myer)

Hosta flowers are not to be despised. *H.* 'Grand Master' flowers shown.

while the opposite destroys it. In addition, a large leaf in the foreground gives us the opportunity of exercising our skills in contrasting shapes and sizes, which we call "texture." Further examples along these lines are the placing of bright colors in the foreground with dim greens and grey-greens in the distance, or shining blades with matte beyond.

Variegation is popular today and the hostas provide us with numerous variations on diverse themes. Variegation in bright colors, particularly yellow, is the equivalent to an exclamation mark in gardens and should not be overdone. It should, I feel, be used when a stimulant is needed—such as a surprise round a corner—and not as a continuously administered cocktail! Yellow variegation is the most telling, both near at hand and also far away where it tends to shorten the perspective; it is most suitable for use with bright or "hot" color associations. White variegation denotes coolness and is best with soft colors such as pinks and mauves. There are today several hostas of soft—sometimes bright—yellowish tone over the whole leafblade. These are most valuable for a variety of color schemes and usually show most yellow coloring in bright light, being a subtle yellowish green in shade. They blend with most colors which are not in the bluish-pink part of the spectrum. Blue-green and glaucous leaves are the exact opposite and add tone to soft color schemes, increase the sense of distance and "cool down" the rich effect of coppery-purple foliage.

But in order to avoid the continuous cocktail idea, foliage of tints other than green should be used sparingly, not as a contrast to each other. Particularly does this apply to white and yellow variegation; their values are so different that they are best kept apart, surrounded by quiet green, and not allowed to compete with each others.

While much of this book is devoted to the craft and science of our subject, my chapter is concerned almost entirely with the art of gardening—the placing of plants and their effect upon their neighbors. Gardening for effect is like making a Christmas pudding: one has to know what ingredients to use and by long stirring and cooking the finished effect will, if sufficient knowledge and skill have been brought to bear, emerge in due course and give delight. Making simply a collection of plants is a different matter, but even those of us who are primarily collectors will usually find, in course of time, that our tastes become educated by the careful placing of plants.

I think we look upon hostas first as foliage plants. There is so much satisfaction to be got out of the contemplation of a goodly hosta clump that it is small wonder that they are becoming so popular. Their

Hostas in a perennial bed. *H.* 'Shade Fanfare' in foreground. Large clump of *H.* 'Sum and Substance' in center. (C. Allen. Courtesy of Klehm Nursery)

flowers are however not to be despised; they vary from white through many shades of pale lilac to purple, and apart from the yellow variegated kinds are therefore fairly easy to place in the garden. In spite of their intrinsic beauty of line and tint, I hear of some gardeners who cut out the flowering stems so that the foliage can be contemplated unalloyed. This I suppose is mainly because of the unfortunate habit some kinds have of retaining their fading flowers. But should we for the same reason eschew delphiniums, gladiolas or some lilies? Compare these all with the *Liatris* species (Gayfeather): is anything so mournful as a spike of flowers which become dead at the top first? Joy never comes unadulterated in this world and even the august camellia hangs on to its dead flowers for too long. Moreover, though many hosta stems may lean one way or another they never need staking, and the different kinds may be had in flower from soon after midsummer until autumn.

Let us look at their flowers first, and imagine a border in full sun except at one end, it may be filled with scarlet phloxes or roses, with perhaps some yellow or orange flowers to add to the scheme, and be backed with or grouped in front of coppery-purple foliage shrub—say cotinus, corylus or prunus. This would be a rich combination and perhaps at one end where the sun does not strike too strongly I would place *Hosta ventricosa* for the sake of its fine, delicately marked, rich purple flowers. Its cultivar, 'Aureomarginata' with cream-edged leaves, would be even more striking, with a foreground planting of *Ajuga reptans* 'Atropurpurea' whose shining carpet of purplish leaves gives rise to short spikes of blue flowers in spring.

Let us now suppose a color scheme of soft, cool colors, pinks and mauves with some grey foliage and white roses. Here *Hosta fortunei* 'Hyacinthia' would contribute lovely grey-green leaves and plentiful pale lavender flowers. Although its leaf coloring is not quite so grey as that of *H. sieboldiana*, its flowers are much superior in color and hold themselves well above the foliage. There are many hostas with lily-shaped, pale lilac flowers, in fact this is the predominant color and shape. It reaches a highlight in *H.* 'Hadspen Blue', one of the compact English *H.* × *tardiana* hybrids with particularly blue-grey leaves. They are surmounted by broad heads of flowers. This is a character to be sought in short growers, we thereby lose the tall stems of many kinds which are bare but for their faded flowers. The cool lilac tints of the many assort easily with most colors, and, being pale, they reveal themselves well at dusk. To my mind, they are particularly pleasing with flowers of pink and purple, and a group of hardy perennials rich in pink tones is that of the astilbes which, like phloxes,

H. 'Hadspen Blue', developed by Eric Smith in England.

prefer cool moist conditions. Here again there is the decided contrast of the broad hosta leaves with the dissected foliage of the astilbes.

We might revert for a moment to the claims of *H. albomarginata*, now to be known as *H. sieboldii*, whose flowers are of the same rich coloring and wide bell-shape of those of *H. ventricosa*. It is a comparatively small species, with erect stems of some 18 in. (45 cm) above the narrow leaves which, in the original form, are edged with white. It is very free flowering. *H. decorata*, which is also usually grown in its white-edged form, has flowers of similar coloring. These both have sufficient rich tinting in the flowers to merit their careful placing—apart from their leaf color—and contrast well with all yellow flowers, such as the paler daylilies and *Lysimachia ciliata*. For planting schemes involving white flowers there are some superlative hostas. Let us start with the comparatively small *H.* 'Ginko Craig'. A planting a yard (.9 m) or so across of its pale green leaves is noticeable through the growing season, and the flowers are produced with great abundance. As a foreground to purple phloxes, or blue hydrangeas, its garden value is undisputed. Apart from *H. sieboldiana* 'Elegans', and new hybrids like *H.* 'Big Mama' and *H.* 'Blue Umbrellas', there are several glaucous varieties with white or palest lilac flowers. Against coppery foliage of berberis or cotinus, they are supreme. But spare a thought for those two admirable green-leafed hybrids *H.* 'Royal Standard' and *H.* 'Honeybells'; in these we have large scented flowers over mounds of lush, shining foliage. This makes them specially suitable for woodland clearings or areas under trees where green is the predominant color, from hardy ferns to glossy dark ground cover of Waldsteinia and London Pride.

But among green-leafed hostas none has the size and magnificence of *H. montana*, sometimes made synonymous with *H. elata*. The great, shining, dark

H. 'Shogun'

The yellow margins of H. *montana* 'Aureo-marginata' gradually turns to white as the season progresses.

green blades are deeply veined and the lilac flowers are borne at the ends of wayward stems. We cannot have a garden without some pure green and it is as well to remind ourselves of this fact. This is where, perhaps as a surprise, we may introduce a white variegated form, which always reveal most white in shade. So far I have seen nothing superior to one of the largest, H. 'Shogun'. I have it placed in front of a soft lilac phlox. Among newer kinds, H. 'Francee' with dark green leaves neatly edged with white is very appealing.

So many are the assets of hostas that I find my mind tavelling back to what I have written, and thoughts come of the common parent of H. 'Honeybells' and H. 'Royal Standard', H. *plantaginea* 'Grandiflora'. This, in those districts which are both moist and warm, treats us to large, scented white flowers in late summer and autumn, when they provide a delightful contrast to pink nerines and Japanese anemones, during the time when their leaves may be turning to pale yellow. It is strange to find a hosta actually needing sunshine in England to hasten its flowers. Earlier in the season its light shining greenery is specially good, as Gertrude Jekyll found, with flowers of bright blue and pale yellow, and this brings us back once again to the importance of our glade of varied greens.

While the general pervading floral color of hostas assorts so well with all the grey and white-variegated kinds, those with yellow variegated leaves are not so easy to place. We should remember that, in contrast to the white-variegated varieties, yellow-striped or flushed leaves color most strongly in full light. This is, culturally, not easy to achieve with shade lovers such as hostas. Some, such as the old H. *fortunei* 'Albopicta' and 'Aurea', turn to green when summer comes. Others may retain their striking yellow variegation in shade or sun; others, again, whose leaves are yellowish all over seem to put up with all but the

hottest sun. The yellow edges of the blue-leafed H. 'Frances Williams' intensify as the season advances, whereas the yellow in the most striking yellow-edged H. *montana* 'Aureomarginata' form will turn gradually with age to white. Much the same occurs with the newer, splendid, green-rimmed, yellow-leafed H. 'Gold Standard'. Add to these facts that practically all yellow-variegated kinds mentioned have pale lilac flowers and my early simile of a cocktail will be the more apparent. If one is going in for careful color blending they are, as I say, not easy to place, but their value in the garden is so great that no amount of care is wasted.

Indeed, the removal of pale, lilac hosta flowers from yellow-leafed forms should be condoned. The color of flower and leaf simply do not "go" together in color scheming; the yellow leaves assort best with any flower whose color is in the strong range between yellow, red and purple. This includes coppery purple foliage, which needs full sun and does not achieve its richest tints in shade. There are many red and orange-tinted lilies which love the same conditions as hostas, and of course there are also the rich purple and the scarlet phloxes already mentioned.

Among newer hostas are several with yellow-flushed, not variegated, leaves and I rank these highly for color work, from the small H. 'Gold Edger' to the larger matte H. 'Piedmont Gold' and glossy H. 'Zounds'. In bright sun they are apt to burn, but in shade their brightness is muted to a clear pale lime-yellow, very valuable as a foil to almost any color. They make a perfect complement to trumpet lilies of yellowish and white coloring and the blue of *Gentian asclepiadea*; this is a hearty perennial for cool, moist places, producing sheaves of blue trumpet flowers in late summer.

It is my feeling that in spring and early summer, all colors are welcome, but that later we take a deeper

H. 'Zounds', a metallic gold that glows at dusk.

One of the most natural of plant groupings is the use of ferns and hostas together. Whatever the color of the hosta leaves, the dainty filigree of most ferns is in direct and delightful contrast, and both classes enjoy the same conditions. Some wonderful combinations of colorings can be made with azaleas and rhododendrons (if the soil is free from lime and suitable). There is scarcely a limit to the scope for color scheming; these shrubs bring us every floral color except true blue, and, believe me, there is a hosta at hand for every contrast or harmony. The sharp reds and oranges of azaleas and some rhododendron species invite the yellow-variegated hostas to join them and the grey-leafed and white-variegated hostas ask to be given the pinks, mauves and purples. And the white? They, too, in their coolness take to heart the dark greens. Then there are irises, while the greater bearded irises enjoy different conditions from those preferred by hostas, there are many of the narrow-leafed groups, the Siberian irises and their relatives for instances, which add to any such grouping as big a contrast of foliage as of flowers; colors range from white and light blue to purple, magenta and white.

interest in grouping. This is partly because late summer flowers tend to last longer in flower; just consider, for instance, hydrangeas, fuchsias, roses, clematises, potentillas and heathers alone. It is when colors of flowers and leaves last long enough to sink into our beings that the urge comes most strongly to treat gardening as an art and not just a craft.

So far many of my remarks have been concerned as much with the value of hosta flowers as with their foliage, and as a consequence late-flowering plants have been cited. But let us now consider late spring and early summer, when the leaves are fresh and shapely, pure and not damaged by storms nor by what I once heard described as "the lesser fauna of the garden."

It was the inclusion of hostas in big groups of shrubs and such plants as the above at Chelsea Show—which is always held in late May—that awakened me to their untold values. They were not only an excellent aid to covering up unsightly sacking, but were valued also as an indispensable complement to the shrubs. And so they are in the garden.

A most natural plant gouping. Shown are *H.* 'Fragrant Bouquet', various clones of *Athyrium nipponicum* and *Hakonechloa macra* 'Aureola'.

The Hosta Book

Hostas dominate in island beds.

While my preference is for large-leafed hostas, we must remember that some people have quite small gardens, yards or patios. Here will be found places for some of the small variants and hybrids, all of them complete replicas of the greater kinds. Such as *H.* 'Shining Tot, with tiny dark green leaves and violet flowers; *H.* 'Gold Edger', a pure yellow-leafed, crisp-looking plant admirable for frontal planning as its name suggests. The contrast in the spring between it and the coppery brown young leaves of *Epimedium* × *rubrum* is an asset to any border, as would be *H.* 'Sea Sprite', yellow finely edged with green, and the white-edged *H.* 'Ginko Craig'.

After what I have written, I hope hostas emerge as plants of invaluable foliage with flowers of delicate, or even great, beauty. My mind goes back to a vivid garden picture, featuring the huge blue-grey, rounded leaves of *Hosta sieboldiana* 'Elegans', set in a big clump, in front of a Copper Beech hedge, with the airy sprays of warm yellow flowers of a shrubby hypericum arching over it. This is the sort of placing which you will discover for yourselves; I am still experimenting with *H.* 'Shade Fanfare'; its delicate creamy green tones seem to me to demand companion flowers of clear yellow. Placing comes, like a Christmas pudding, from knowing how to mix and cook . . . , but remember that hostas do not thrive in

frost pockets. Though spring frost will not injure the flower stalks deep down among the leaves, the latter may get spoiled and hostas do not throw up later crops of foliage. Slugs and snails should be warned off, if possible, and notices put up to deter mice from removing flower buds and seedpods. Other than these little troubles, your hostas are likely to thrive if given suitable thought.

Tiny *H.* 'Shining Tot', sunproof, pest-resistant, stoloniferous and rugged.

Vigor, for example, is largely a function of the DNA found in the mitochondria. If the maternal (pod) parent contributes most of the mitochondria to the first cell of the new individual, the paternal (pollen) contribution doesn't seem to be a significant factor in the vigor department. The same is true of color plastid inheritance. The pod parent (female) supplies virtually all of the plastids, found in the large cytoplasm regions of the egg cell, together with the food to sustain the first days of the new individual. The contribution to color inheritance by the pod parent is more than unequal, it is overpowering, with only a very few exceptions.

The consequence of the maternal inheritance of color common in plants is of great importance to the hybridizer: do not expect variegated offspring from a non-variegated pod parent. A further implication is that the rule of Mendelian genetics, built on the premise of equal contributions by both male and female parents (or pollen and pod) does not hold up when predicting variegated offspring. The few exceptions are probably caused by the influence of the pollen nucleus chromosomes, acting with the pod nucleus chromosomes to influence plastid expression. They "help to control the environment" surrounding the plastids, but the presence of DNA in the plastids makes them almost autonomous in pigment programming. This all leads to the inevitable premise that THE FEMALE DOES MORE—a statement which brings to the author's ears the sound of some copies of this book being slammed shut. However, the evidence is clear, when tens of thousands of seedlings are grown from seed taken from a plain, green plant, the level of consistency in seedling color is something to behold. This is true even when a wide assortment of variegated pollen parents are used to produce the seed. After this explanation, the reader can supply the prediction of the chances of getting variegated offspring from two non-variegated parents.

A notable exception is the quite rare phenomenon called "sporting," an aberration that seem to occur spontaneously, almost like magic. Many of the unusual dwarf conifers originated as natural "sports," for example. The technicians who tissue-culture plants tell me that unusual forms or "sports" are more likely to occur in older cultures, almost as if mistakes in replicating cells are more likely in more mature individuals. Tissue culture propagators are obliged, in their quest to maintain clonal integrity, to start with fresh ex-plants from the original source plant after the "soup," or source of ex-plants, begins to age, a condition in which "accumulated mistakes" in genetic programming result in an increased number of mutations.

The "sporting" game seems to follow a law of probability, which says that cell duplications are NOT like "copier" copies all of the time. The more copies made, the greater the likelihood that a slight deviation from the norm of duplication will occur and grows geometrically with time. Also, it is worth mentioning, for readers not in the measurement business, that error in measurements and processes is something that you can depend on, given a large sample-size. Thus measurements in scientific work are usually expressed with a $\pm$ value after the number value to indicate the range of expected error. While we do not flinch at the thought of human error and even expect it, the estimate often quoted of an average of one error in 30 human calculations, many of us cling to the myth of infallibility of man-made devices like computers. While it is true that computer calculations are less likely to result in errors by a factor on the order of one million times, it may be of some comfort to know that even computer processors make errors. It may be a further comfort to know that inanimate objects like iron crystals, for example, also tend to be imperfect in their geometric pattern. Perfect iron crystals, extremely rare, exhibit a tremendous increase in strength, as compared to run-

Some variegated sports of the plain blue hosta, *H. sieboldiana* 'Elegans' under evaluation.

A sport with very little chlorophyll. Still to be determined is whether the sport, when separated from the mother plant, can prosper under average garden condition.

H. 'Great Expectations'

of-the-mill crystals commonly found.

The probability of change over time (number of generations) provides the basis for seeking "sports" in older, undisturbed clumps or plants which have been propagated for decades. For example, a very exciting sport of *H. sieboldiana* 'Elegans' was recently discovered in a long row of very mature clumps. While the mother plant is bluish in the spring with large round leaves, the sport, to be called *H.* 'Great Expectations' has a wide, irregular blue margin with a yellow center. The chances are that the sport, with less chlorophyll, will not grow as large as the original mother plant, but its color pattern may offer a valuable addition to the shade garden.

In an attempt to understand the dynamics of living plant cells, some recently discovered phenomena should be mentioned. **Living organisms carry at least four times more gene-programming potential than they use at any given time.** While the switching-on or switching-off of a particular genetic program is only dimly understood, there is ample evidence that it occurs. Two examples will suffice: 1) Greying of

H. 'Golden Sunburst', a sport of H. 'Frances Williams' in back and to the left of the statuary. (Garden of R. J. Myer)

hair with time. In some ways, you can say that we become more variegated as we grow older. A similar development occurs in plants. Their best variegation is reached at maturity. 2) Decrease in human muscle strength with age. For reasons which are not clear, there are fewer energy-producing mitochondria in older cells. A similar development occurs in mature plants. Their vigor and rate of growth decreases after they have reached maturity. The concept that cells use different parts of their genetic programming at different times in different environments is well accepted, even if it is destabilizing. It is worth noting that germ cells seem to have a method of self-regulation that gives them the ability to transfer traits to the next generation with relatively few and minor deviations.

Twisted scape "sport" under evaluation. Among other considerations, is it stable or desirable?

Many examples of "sports" enriching our selection of plants are a part of the folklore of horticulture, but visions of wealth and fame for the "discoverer" are usually short-lived. Most usually, a new color combination disappears as the season progresses, or in the following year or in a few years. Suggestion: wait at least four years before "crowing" about your sport. Compare adjacent divisions, as well as adjacent leaves. Compare older leaves with newer ones. Compare what you see now with photographs taken in prior years. While there are notable exceptions, it is safe to say that **the more complex the color pattern, the more likely the pattern will shift in time.** This is particularly true with **medio-variegation,** or splashes or streaks of color in the center of the leaf. So, if you grow enough plants and wait long enough, you will eventually see plants like *H. tokudama* 'Aureo-Nebulosa' throw off a blue division which is identical to *H. tokudama* and even see a golden sport of *H.* 'Frances Williams.' While relatively rare, variegated

Fasciated scape "sport" tentatively named, *H.* 'Backscratcher'.

small price to pay for the extra beauty of variegated plants.

Those of us who have tried to "touch up" a nick in the finish of our car discover that matching colors is a craft in its own right. In the printing or dyeing business, despite careful quality control, often elusive factors, including the purity and concentration of the dye or ink compounds, the concentration of the catalysts used, the pH and the temperature of the mixture may frustrate the realization of the desired product or may later fade to an unacceptable degree. Clearly then, the nature of color in mechanical things, as distinguished from living organisms, is a complex matter.

But the forming of color in living cells makes the processes involved in color printing look simple. It is no accident that gold hostas look brighter or yellow margins become more creamy as the intensity of the light builds during the summer. It is no accident that the foliage of hostas grown in sandy soils with high metal content produce more luxuriant and vivid colors. A simple thing like holding back on watering will make the red in red flowers look more intense. Litmus is not alone as an indicator pigment whose color varies with soil conditions. It is no accident that blue hosta typically appear bluer in cooler areas, and particularly near bodies of water. All of these plant differences will give the reader a clue as to the experience(s) those of us who routinely observe a given clone in different parts of the country have to deal with. We may express delight, surprise or occasionally, disappointment with the differences. But what we are really seeing is the influence of **microenvironment.**

plants do 'sport' back to plain forms, which have more chlorophyll and so are more efficient in producing food. This phenomenon is not restricted to the genus, *Hosta*, as it is true in all plant genera which occasionally develop aberrations such as variegation, and indeed, is generally true of almost all mutations.

When one wanders into an area used as a nuclear or chemical dump site and sees all sorts of "weird" plants, little mental effort is required to make the connection between radiation or chemical exposure and mutation rate. The shifts in expression may be to a plain form or an even more exotic form than formerly existed. Obviously, the new exotic form should not have the same name. The fact that plants will change is statistically predictable, largely the result of the fact that plant cells are in a **dynamic** life process. The plant breeder may have to give up a breeding line because it reverts to a plain form or he may discover a stable mutant. But, he should expect reversion to the plain form to occur far more frequently than a stable new form. Removing an occasional, wayward division is a

Double-flower "sport" under evaluation.

Attending carefully, anyone can note slight differences within the same clone within a single garden. Soils vary in their metal and mineral content, acidity, temperature and the amounts of water they can hold, even within the confines of a small garden. Further, closely adjacent areas vary drastically in levels of shade. Part of the satisfaction found in working with hostas is the ease with which they can be moved from site to site, and so maximize their beauty by locating a particularly suitable microenvironment. You may find, as other gardeners have, that experimentation pays off.

If the world of "magic" is ruled out, how can one account for the appearance of variegated "sports" in a non-variegated plant? It must be assumed that non-green plastids existed before any variegation was evident in the cell. The fact that the molecular structures of green and non-green genes are so similar makes it likely that a switch of only one or two atoms in the green gene results in a non-green gene. The green gene is thought to be dominant, while the non-green gene is recessive. In such situations, only the green is expressed when both genes are present. Green plant's cells checked under the microscope clearly proves the presence of plastids of other colors, which is not at all unusual. If somehow, during active growth, in meristemic regions where very few cells are involved in the active growth process, the dominant gene (green in this case) is segregated out in a suitable meristemic layer responsible for a particular leaf region, then the non-green gene gets a chance to assert itself in that region.

Trying to explain how a fuzzy color-potpourri, as is often observed when variegated hosta leaves first emerge from the ground, develop into a leaf possessing distinct color regions or multiple colors seems to call for some kind of focusing lense, to bring order out of the melange. But alas, there are no lenses in plant cells. That focusing or localization of color variegation occurs during the process of repeated cell divisions. The division or separating or "segregation" process eventually leads to groups of cells possessing a single color plastid. If the group of cells stems from a "non-green" gene, the color can be seen, as "green" is not around to suppress it.

How can one explain why adjacent, medio-variegated leaves vary from each other and other leaves within the hosta clump? As growth is a dynamic process, it is subject to the availability and concentration of raw materials, energy, enzymes and hormones. At any instant, the cell population growth behavior in a particular region of a leaf may vary from that in the same region of an adjacent leaf. This is particularly noticeable with medio-variegation, which include streaks or blotches in the center of the leaf. Basically, the reason that adjacent leaves, with the complex medio-variegation, are not likely to be "carbon copies" of each other is the variance in their microenvironments.

How can one account for changes in variegation during the same year? Just as different members of an orchestra may be participating more or less actively, so the activity in growth of plastids can vary. In the spring, for example, some hosta cultivars may show beautiful variegation or good color for only 3–6 weeks. Examples include *H. fortunei* 'Viridis-marginata', *H.* 'Chartreuse', *H.* 'Sharmon', and *H. ventricosa* 'Aureo-maculata'. These cultivars undoubtedly possess at least two differently colored plastids. The conditions of spring growth allow the 'colorful' plastids to grow more rapidly than the plain green plastids. As the season wears on, the green plastid begins to grow at a faster rate. Within a few weeks, green wins the race. The beauty now is plainer.

A double sport that includes margin-stitching and center variegation induced by radiation, *H.* 'Embroidery'.

Variegation shown lasts for six weeks in the spring before a uniform blue sets in. This seedling was never named.

This behavior leads to the breeder's standard that good variegated foliage should display consistent variegation throughout the growing season. A "lock-step discipline" is required of all the plastids to grow at the same rate. This is especially critical in more complex, variegation patterns. It further helps to explain why perfect "rubber-stamping" of variegation is entirely improbable. The worth of a complex variegation finally hinges on the degree to which the norm of variegation is maintained, or how attractive the deviations are as part of the mound, particularly when seen from a normal viewing distance.

Sooner or later, someone (probably a child) will inquire about the mechanics of the variegation pattern. If we were to construct a model, offering a working explanation and agreed with what is known, we might say, "When a new plant typically starts out as a rather unsophisticated, single cell, the struggling male nucleus and the patient female ova have just merged their assets to set up a new entity. What's a lonely cell to do by itself? One begets two, two beget four and so on." Plants, however, are not single-celled bacteria. They have complicated requirements, so need specialized parts. Just as the human brain develops from a particular region of a particular layer of the human embryo and just as the human skeleton emerges from another particular region of another particular layer, so it is that the parts of the leaf emerge from particular regions of embryonic (germ) layers. There are 3 layers, just as there are in the human embryo. We refer to the 3 layers as L-1, L-2 and L-3.

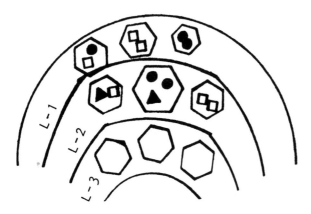

Diagram showing embryonic cell layers in hostas where most active growth by cell division takes place.

There are many cells in each layer, but only 3 or 4 cells are doing all the work, the work of growing and dividing. The outside L-1 layer is responsible for the top layer or epidermis of the leaf and is particularly responsible for the leaf margin. Variegated margins come from the colored plastids in at least some of the active cells of L-1.

L-2 cells are largely responsible for the greater part of the mid-leaf. Medio-variegation involves some colored, active cells from the L-2 layer. Imagine the traffic problems involved in trying to transport the same amount of water, raw materials, enzymes and growth hormones to insure uniform growth to all of these "active" cells, and so insure a uniform variegation pattern.

We know that margin-type variegations are more stable than medio-types. The active colored plastid cells in L-1 must experience a more constant environment than their neighbors in the L-2 region. In a way, it's like comparing the front row of marching soldiers with the second row. Even if one in the front line either falls out of step, or slows down, or moves sideways slightly, the front line continues to move. The second row can be "sabotaged" more easily, by either a change in the front or third row.

Margin-type variegation, such as *H*. 'Fringe Benefit', is more stable than medio-types.

It is also possible for an active, colored plastid cell in L-1 to become inactive by "losing" its place within the layer or even shift to L-2. Not only can the L-2 active, colored plastids cell lose its place within the layer, it can shift to either L-1 or L-3, introducing a new color in a different region. If you can't memorize all of that, it's easy enough to pass out copies or cassettes.

At this point, if you can still recall the title of this chapter, you are probably wondering about the connection between variegation and hybridization. Well, as variegated hosta cultivars outsell single-color plants by about 10:1, at least one reasonable goal for hybridizing hostas is to develop superior, variegated clones. John Elsley makes the point, in his chapter,

"Diversity of Hosta" that variegation is no longer enough. Mr. Elsley, as does Mr. Yoshimichi Hirose in his chapter, refers to breeding goals. Attributes like "new", "unique", "better", a "particular problem-solver" all are easy to articulate, but difficult to achieve. Successful breeding obviously involves more than brushing pollen and planting seed, especially if the breeder expects to produce plants which have long-term, commercial value. It is obvious to a nurseryman that marketability and customer satisfaction are likely to coincide if the plant possesses vigor, another worthy breeding goal. It would be nice to report that the biggest sellers are the very same plants found in the 100-year-old gardens, but unhappily, that is not the case. Hosta hybridizing is still in its "glory" period, with only a small portion of genetic potential of the genus tapped. The genus still is open to committed hybridizers, which could be an introduction to the subject of hybridizing.

Randomness implies the absence of guidance by a governing mind, eye, objective, or the like. No comprehensible plan, program or sense of control is evident. Events are at the mercy of chance. That is *not* what hybridizing is about. It's safe to say that bees go about their business in a random way as they pollinate flowers. There are human beings who are trying to do consciously what we think the bees do unconsciously. Working hybridizers, both amateur and professional, must believe that humans can "beat the bees," can do better than that random process. Scientists understand that energy in a particular direction is required to upset the laws of chance. Some people would also argue that *hubris* is necessary.

The fact that over 99.99% of all hybridizers are amateurs, a word incidentally, whose root is "love," who undertake their breeding programs without the stimulus or prospect of monetary reward. This, in no way, indicates a lack of expertise or accomplishment. This is true, whether the amateur breeder is working with Arabian stallions on a grand scale or with *Hosta* in a small backyard. Nor does it imply that the small-scale hybridizer, lacking institutional, corporate or wealthy patronage backing, is a mere dabbler, seeking trifles to relieve boredom. One curious fact— there are more male than female hybridizers. It is no secret that many of the best ideas, discoveries, and inventions have been born in small settings. The idea that whole industries started in someone's basement or garage should not surprise anyone. Hybridizing in one's backyard remains one arena where tremendous startup investments are not a requisite to realize great personal pride and satisfaction. It is quite appropriate that small-scale hybridizers have performed a key part in making hostas as useful, attractive and as popular as they are.

Like most happenings, the recent surge of interest in hostas did not stem from a single event. Words like "timing" and "confluence" come to mind. The first three parts of the puzzle are best described as trends. As the cost of land has increased over the decades, new homes were built on smaller plots (a good reason to breed for smaller hostas). This in turn meant that fewer, but choicer plants made sense. Simultaneously, the availability of "cheap" labor to care for extensive, labor-intensive gardens was drying up. The third trend was the rising interest in time devoted to recreation and vacationing. This trend heightened demand for less fussy plants which demanded less time and attention, and could be expected to "fend for themselves" in the garden. The fact that professional collectors were sending hostas to England, Holland, Germany and the United States for over 100 years from Japan, Korea and China also helped. At the least, it furnished large arboreta and private collectors some experience in growing hostas.

An epoch-making event, in 1922, was the development of the techniques for cloning new plants from single cells (micropropagation or tissue-culture). Every cell possesses the genetic programming needed to form a complete organism, so the key problem was discovering and defining a suitable environment and stimulus for the programming to operate. The possiblity of producing enough numbers of a choice, rare and expensive plant to place it within the reach of, not just the wealthy connoisseur/collector, but the average gardener as well, is now closer to reality.

Enough gardeners were growing hostas by the 1960s to make the organization of the American

An epoch-making event was the development of the technique for cloning plants from single cells, called tissue-culture or micropropagation.

Hosta Society in 1968 a reality. This occurred at a time when most gardeners still referred to hostas as "funkias." The Society, not only took in the charge of educating the public about the name, but also on the landscape uses of the genus. They also worked out an arrangement with the Landscape Arboretum at the University of Minnesota to serve as Registrar for new cultivars. Photographs of some of the better *Hosta* species began to appear, not only in the *The American Hosta Society's Journal,* but also in gardening and horticultural magazines and books such as *American Horticulturist, Horticulture, Flower and Garden,* Brooklyn Botanic Garden's booklet on *Shade Gardening,* and Time-Life's *Easy Gardening* in the United States, as well as publications produced in England, Holland, Germany and Sweden. All this attention was lavished on plants, whose available stocks, in many cases, were miniscule. The plants pictured were mostly those imported by small-scale collectors or developed by small-scale hybridizers. Many gardeners must have seen and been intrigued by those pictures, for the hosta scene has never been the same since.

The interest created in plants, most of which were not generally available, was soon to be satisfied. A few nurserymen, possessed of enough capital and confidence in the future of hostas, undertook to make the plants more readily available. By the mid-1970s, catalogs with good descriptions and colored illustrations of *Hosta* cultivars, at dramatically reduced prices appeared. The need for education continues, but the fact that large numbers of gardeners at least recognize the names, some of the features and uses of hostas helps mightily. The same story might have been written for many other genera, "still waiting to be discovered." Ultimately, much of the credit must be given to the hosta plants themselves and to the backyard hybridizers who developed them.

Mass hosta propagation at the Klehm Nursery in Illinois.

THE TECHNIQUE OF HYBRIDIZING

Bees' appetite for pollen is well placed, for it is a high-grade protein, laced with a rich variety of other nutrients. It seems more than fortuitous that the hardworking bee is busy among the flowers from the time ambient temperature permits its enzymes to carry on normal functions early in the morning to that time in the late afternoon when the temperature falls below the level that permits optimum enzyme efficiency. Or one might hypothesize that the bee quits late in the day because it is tired, or is having trouble seeing, or the pollen is not in good condition by the late afternoon. The last theory leads to the observation that hybridizers must harvest pollen at the right time.

The species in many animal as well as plant groups can go on without the separate male. The example of agamospermy in *H. ventricosa* by Dr. Jones has already been cited. A hosta flower typically has one female receptor, the stigma and many male (pollen) generators, the brush-like anthers, which generally surround the stigma. If you nip the filament holding a pollen-bearing anther at different times of day and brush it against a piece of white paper, you can see a number of differences. Generally, the pollen is best when the bees are most active, about mid-morning, although it does vary with individual flowers in various parts of the garden.

Scanning electron micrograph of a pollen grain of Hosta kiyosumiensis, x1200 magnification. (By M. Chung and Dr. S. B. Jones, Jr., University of Georgia)

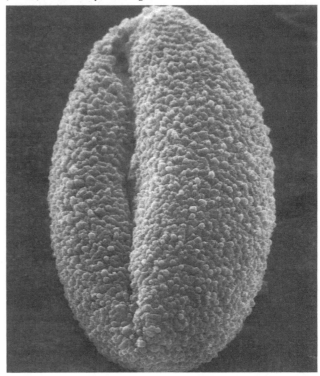

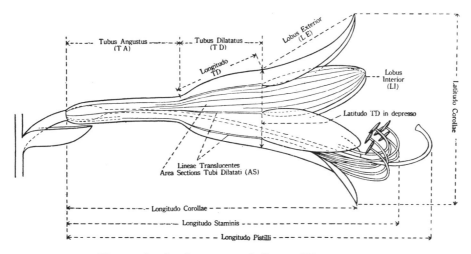

Diagram showing the sex parts of a flower of *Hosta*.

A certain minimum amount of heat is needed for the pollen to ripen, or to reach a condition in which it can be transferred as that powder-like material we call pollen grains. Generally speaking, the optimum temperature is between 65–85°F (18–29°C), with 75°F (24°C) being the probable optimum. As the temperature moves into higher ranges, pollen structure and viability deteriorates rapidly. Assuming that the flower you have chosen to be the pollen parent has produced functioning pollen, there is the task of gathering it either at the right time, which means competing with the bees, or gathering it a bit earlier, before the bees have started their rounds. The pollen-bearing anthers should be taken indoors (out of ultraviolet or natural light) at once and allowed to warm up to the right temperature before harvesting the pollen.

Storing Pollen for Later Use Some people use gelatin capsules, now rather difficult to get in certain areas, to store pollen. A 3″ × 5″ (7.5 × 12.5 cm) white paper (low grade) pad works fine. First make 2 folds so that you have 3 sections of 1″ × 5″ (2.5 × 12.5 cm); Brush the excess pollen into the middle section, over-lap the top and bottom and then fold in the sides so that you have an envelope about 1″ × 3″ (2.5 × 7.5 cm). Store in a refrigerator (not the freezer) and chances are the pollen will "work" for the rest of the year as well into the early part of next year.

Preparing the Pod Parent Emasculation of flowers is relatively easy to carry out. The trick is timing, late afternoon of the day before the flower will open, that is while it is still in bud, is the time you must do it. Carefully slit the bud open to expose, but not damage the sexual parts, trim away the petals and sepals, depriving insects of a landing platform, then locate the 6 (brush-like) pollen-sacs (anthers) and without hesitation, snip them away without

damaging the female stigma. The odds are that you have in one bold action eliminated the possibility of self-pollination as well as insect pollination. As *Hosta* pollen is too heavy for wind to be a serious factor, you can look forward to the next day with some degree of confidence.

Making the Cross(es) Acting as a marriage broker, you are not only introducing 2 hostas to each other, you are also determining which will play the role of female. My neighbors have often seen me brushing pollen at two hour intervals, starting before the bees have reported for duty, on the day that the flower opened, as well as the evening before, and after the pod parent's flower was emasculated. It takes about 90 minutes for the pollen to travel to the ovary where fertilization takes place. The stigma, which enlarges somewhat and is moist when it is most receptive to pollen, is brushed with a small camel or sable hair brush carrying the pollen, or the anther with filament as a handle, loaded with viable pollen (it should look powdery when tapped on a piece of paper). Two gentle swipes with the brush should be more than sufficient.

Examples of Cross(es) 1. Parent "A" has green leaves with a crimped edging; medium-sized clump; dwarf; poorly-formed flowers on branching flower scapes; and a background of a yellow grandparent with red petioles. Parent "B" has large mounds; bright yellow, glossy, sun-tolerant leaves; fragrant, well-formed, large flowers; and from the same yellow grandparent with red petioles. The crosses are "A" × "B" and "B" × "A". Of the 2,000 seedlings at the 4 leaf stage, all but 20 are snipped out. The "chosen" include some very small, others large, bright yellow seedlings, with early signs of crimped edging and red petioles. At the 10 leaf stage, the best 10 are chosen to be grown on for 4 years, hoping to yield plants with large size mounds; glossy, bright yellow color leaves, crimped along the edges; with red petioles; sun-tolerant; and branching scapes with large, well-formed, fragrant flowers. The chances are that the best of the 10 must be crossed again and again, before the goal is fully realized.

Large scape leaves, together with a large fragrant flower offers an instant corsage, a worthwhile goal. Seedling shown is under evaluation.

Flower-like buds of good color, attractive well before the appearance of the flower is a worthwhile goal.

The thickly-set, scape leaves, making a rosette-like flower, make the appearance of this seedling's flower on anticlimax.

2. Parent "C" is small clump; medio-variegation (unstable), light blue, glossy leaves that self-shed (any debris that falls on them); and sun-tolerant with poor, light blue flowers. Parent "D" is a medium clump; with dark blue, cupped, puckered leaves; and flowers small, but fragrant, nicely placed on the scape in radial fashion. "C" and "D" are cousins. Only the "C" × "D" cross is made, to increase the likelihood of variegated seedlings. At the 4 leaf stage, six selections exhibit either margin or medio-variegations, light blue favored, glossy, self-shedding, small leaves. At the 10 leaf stage, the best 4 are chosen to be grown on for 4 years, hoping to see the smallest, light blue with stable variegation; sun-tolerant; self-shedding leaves and well-formed, nicely spaced, fragrant flowers. The "blue" sought must not depend solely on the indumentum, but have a good blue base color below the indumentum, to insure a longer-lasting color.

3. Parent "E" has vigor; large size; unstable variegation with streaks of white in the center; sun-tolerance; and well-formed, densely-packed flower racemes that bloom in late June. Parent "F" has little vigor; small to medium size; stable variegation of white-centers with 2-tone, green margins; and few, but well-formed, fragrant flowers. Only the "E" × "F" cross is made, to increase the prospects of vigorous seedlings. "E" and "F" are second cousins. At the 4 leaf stage, 4 selections show white-centered variegation with wide, irregular green margins. At the 10 leaf stage, the 3 most vigorous are selected to be grown on for 4 years, hoping to see the largest seedling with white-centered, stable variegation; sun-tolerance; and abundant, well-formed, early-blooming, fragrant flowers. Flower arrangers, have indicated their preference for white-centered foliage, which limits the chloroplasts present, which limits the vigor. The chances are that the final seedling selected will start growth in the spring with chartreuse centers, which gradually turn to white as the season progresses.

Labeling Use a small, weatherproof tag, or one that defies wind, rain, sun or the hands of little children. Using a soft, lead pencil, or any of the water-proof pencils or inks available, write first the name of the pod parent, then "×" for crossed by, and followed by the name of the pollen parent. If it looks like rain, make a "dunce" cap out of 6 in. (1.5 cm) square of aluminum foil, shaped by pressing over a pencil point. Then, place the cap over the stigma and gently press the bottom of the cap around the style supporting the stigma. Capping, together with removal of the petals and sepals during emasculation is about all of the protection you will need from accidental insect intrusions. If the pod parent's flower is very small, a very small bag placed over the flower and secured on the flower stem (perhaps by the tie of the label) may work better.

Harvesting the Crop You will know when the seed (fruit) has fully ripened, for the capsule will start to split. About 6 weeks are required from germination to harvesting. The trick is to gather the seed before they scatter. Do not use plastic bags, but rather plain, brown, sandwich, paper bags. After all the seed capsules from a particular pod parent (particular cross) are dropped into a bag, seal the bag with a paper clip, write the name and the cross and "file." Leave plenty of air space in the bag, so the seed capsule may open fully. The individual seeds can be released by gentle stroking with a pencil point after 2 weeks.

Hosta seed capsules, not quite ripened. If capsule cover shows variegation, probability of variegated seedlings is greater.

Storage Separate the hulls of the seed capsule from the seed with a pencil point as noted above. Allow the seed to dry somewhat in a cool, dry place for about a day before replacing in the bag, and sealing with a clip for storage either in a cool, dry place or possibly a working refrigerator (not the freezer section), if storing more than 3 weeks is contemplated. The actual "shelf-life" of *Hosta* seed varies tremendously, but these guidelines have worked well for most situations in an amateur environment. A number of important crosses, such as those with large fragrant flowers, can only be successfully germinated if the period between harvesting and planting is a month or less.

Planting Seed For a species to continue, it must be able to reproduce. Otherwise, the line ends with the individual. The survival of flowering plants depends on obtaining the energy to flower and produce seed. The energy necessary to produce the seed is many times the energy required to produce a flower. The setting for seed production includes a whole host of conditions. Adequate light, for light is the source of energy for all plants and animals. Equally important is access to water, air and nutrients available in a temperature range at which the plant's enzymes can function. Add to this the need to remain sufficiently intact, to be able to function—in short to avoid being devoured by pests, seen or unseen. Add to this the requirements of the embryo within that seed—no placenta or mother's milk is available. Instead, the right range of moisture, the right timing, and some food must be built into the seed which must then fall in a spot where the right quantity of air, temperature and supplementary food can be found before the potential of the seed can be realized to continue the species. Let this recitation serve as a conscious background in planting seed, with the hope that the gardener can improve on the conditions usually found in nature.

Most gardeners prefer to plant seed in a special, protected bed, which is shady, usually a frame filled with a sterile mix of equal parts of perlite and fine sphagnum peat moss (or Jiffy-Mix), thoroughly mixed and moist, but not soggy. Set the seed in rows 2 in. (5 cm) apart, 1 in. (2.5 cm) apart within the row, mist slightly and then cover the entire frame with glass or polyethylene sheeting. Allow at least 1 in. of air space between the seed and the frame cover. Note that the seed is not covered with medium under these conditions. The root (hypocotyl) will appear first followed by the stem (epicotyl). You may have to make a small hole with a match stick and set the root in the soil if it cannot seat itself. Light is not needed until the true leaves appear, but a temperature in the range of 60–75°F (16–24°C) for a period of 10–20 days is absolutely required. Good results can also be had by planting in open soil in the fall and covering with about 2 in. (5 cm) of leaves which do not compact (like oak leaves). If planted in open soil, it is a good idea to cover the seedbed with a screening of ⅜ in. (1 cm) hardware cloth, or coarse burlap, to avoid problems with birds and squirrels.

Artificial Lighting Hosta seedlings are often grown indoors during the winter with a relatively, simple facility providing heat and light. That said, let the author and the reader reach an understanding before either you or I go any further. In the future, if an irate spouse, who may feel shortchanged by the reader's "light" experience with hosta seedlings, threatens me, it is all right for me to say that "I'm sure that we have never met, but where can I find out about these funkias?" So, starting as early as late October to as late as the middle of May (on Long Island), you will have an excuse not to take long vacations or trips. The "little darlings" (hosta seedlings) need you. Another proviso, watering becomes more critical indoors, particularly if you do not own an automatic growth chamber. The same is true of pest problems, largely because they prosper quite well indoors, in the absence of the normal predators and unfavorable conditions they face outdoors. There are some obvious advantages, such as having the plants closer to working level, without the usual "stooping," a boon to the handicapped or people with bad backs. The greatest plus, in this process, is "being there," from the seed to the final siting in the garden.

If a place is located, away from heavy human-traffic, away from house plants, away from plants that are brought indoors from the garden, with access to electrical outlets and water, having good ventilation and a floor surface that won't cause grief, if it gets wet or dirty, and where the temperature is normally at 65–85°F (18–29°C) during the winter, the rest is easy. Commercial flourescent fixtures, 48 in. (130 cm) with 2 or more tubes and supported by adjustable chains are a widely available, cheap and effective light source for this project. A 24 hour timer, to regulate for 14–16 hours of light/day is also worth the small cost. Chloroplasts can only use wavelengths in the red and blue range, and while many, expensive, flourescent bulbs are offered, "Cool White" bulbs are quite adequate at minimum cost. The throw-away, aluminum baking tins (in "loaf" size), about 2.5 in. (5.6 cm) deep, 8.75 in. (22 cm) long, 4 in. (20 cm) wide, that can be inserted into a thin, polyethylene vegetable bag, will last many years at low cost. Pierce the bottom with a fork so as to allow for drainage, as well as allow for air to get to the root hairs. Aluminum wire mesh, often used as rain gutter guards, can be cut into 1 in. (2.5 cm) × 10 in. (25 cm) strips and stapled to the sides, in the mid-region of the pan, so as to make a support to keep the polyethylene bag from resting on the seedlings. Polyethylene is particularly useful because it allows the passage of respiration gases, but not water molecules, thus the need for watering or lifting the bag at the early stages is minimized. Oily film on the bag impedes gas transfer and is easily removed by washing in lukewarm water. Gentle bottom heat may help germination in difficult cases. When growth starts, adjust the bulbs so that they are about 2 in. (5 cm) from the tops of the plant. You will be regularly raising the light fixture as growth proceeds. Regulate the light with a timer so that the plants get at least 14 hours of light per day. Having plants during most of

the winter can be a joy, but plants in the early stages need careful watching and adjustments to take care of their needs. In most cases, it will still require 2 summers before the seedlings bloom.

Closeup of the dense, full, long-lasting flower racemes of *H.* 'Blue Angel', a worthwhile goal in breeding.

Initial Evaluation When each plant has developed 4 leaves, you may choose, with the help of a magnifying glass, to decide which plants are not worth growing on. A small-scissor-snip just below the root-stem junction will thin out your crop. It is at this stage that the need and value of having the best parents available becomes apparent. Consider a final goal of keeping no more than 3% of all of the seedlings; leaving the best 10% at the four-leaf stage helps to avoid problems caused by overcrowding later on. The key question becomes, which are chosen to live?

Large, flat, fragrant flowers, radially arranged on branching scapes, definitely a worthwhile goal in breeding. *H.* 'Fragrant Candelabra' shown.

Although I am considered to be a "successful" hybridizer, whatever that is, do not assume that sure-fire formulas abound. In many ways, we are involved with an art, rather than a scientific process, well tempered by experience, knowledge of the parents, and the new combination of the parental gene pool that is worth seeking. Certainly, the element of luck cannot be overlooked, illustrated by a plant with unstable variegation developing divisions that remain stable. Garden visitors, to a large extent, define my goals in hybridizing. Visitors are confronted with plant-rating questionnaires, as well as extended questions in conversation, all slanted to identify a niche, or which gardening problems require a plant solution, a plant that does not now exist, another way of saying that the plant has "to earn its keep." Lecture and travel schedules help the author determine what is available, the basis for deciding what is unique? Summing up, two background factors emerge in evaluation: 1) What new, desirable combination is sought from the particular parents chosen? 2) Can a "unique" quality be recognized at a very early, 4-leaf stage?

Lighting After the 4-leaf stage, adjust the lighting units so that they are always 2–5 in. (5–12.5 cm) above the growing tips. Also, after the 4-leaf stage, remove the polyethylene covering.

Watering Water needs will vary with temperature, ventilation and rate of growth. Use a fine spray or watering, slow enough, so as not to dislodge the seedlings or compact the soil, but sufficient that the entire soil mass is moistened, but not soggy. When water appears at the bottom drain holes, that's enough. Good drainage in the container cannot be overstressed. If you use peat pots, water is needed when the color starts to turn a light brown. In the early stages, plan on checking water needs every 2 days. A thin sprinkling of perlite on the surface will curb "damping-off." A few drops of saturated soapy water/quart of water will not only act as a "wetting agent," insuring greater absorption of water, but also will help to control any buildup of surface moss. Make sure there is air circulation in the area and provision is made for excess water to drain off. Air at the root level is just as important as water, particularly at the early stages.

Feeding Use a soluble, complete fertilizer (Ex. Peters, Miracle-Gro etc.) approximately 1/10th to 1/20th recommended dosage with each watering. Feed only enough to promote vigor, but maintain slow growth—rapid growth often induces pest problems. Aphids, fungus gnats and red spider mites can be a serious problem indoors, so inspect the underside of leaves frequently for potential pests, while they are few in number (See "Competitors in the Garden").

Hardening Off This is the trickiest operation of all. Laying the groundwork for moving plants outdoors, keep plants in the dark and without water for at least 2 days. For about a week, use or improvise a "cold frame," in which the plant is adapted to greater amounts of wind, light and cooler temperature slowly. If a polyethylene or plastic cover is used, make a hole in it ever larger, over a period of a week. Careful attention to watering is critical. On Long Island (southeastern New York State), the timing for placing plants out of doors is May 10 or later. A month after the last frost-date is safe in other areas. If you can set the plants into moisture-retentive soil in rows at least 18 in. (45 cm) apart and at least 8 in. (20 cm) apart within the row in the late, late afternoon when there is a chance for a soft rain, the plants will thank you.

Seeds from Bee-pollinated Hosta Plants Such seeds which probably derive their genetic materials from one or more parents, are a lot less work, but also a lot less rewarding. It may seem odd, at first glance, that practically none of the issue from random-pollination is even noticed or enters the marketplace. If the pod parent is blue, the offspring tend to be less blue. If the pod parent had a colored-margin, the offspring are almost invariably plain. For example, of 15,000 naturally germinated seedlings from the yellow-margin, *H.* 'Frances Williams,' only one variegated seedling resulted. The energy and space investment in growing naturally germinated seedlings, as judged by the degree of recognition or the number of useful garden plants was never recovered. And to add insult to injury, proctically all of the seedlings were inferior to the original pod parent. It is almost as if succeeding generations were going downhill.

Few of us are so jaded that we are not repeatedly excited by the emergence of a new life from a seed, whether the seed handled its own affairs through a winter out-of-doors, or received a little help in a paper bag stored indoors. The special burden of the hybridizer is to be an extremely selective, even fickle, admirer of life. Swamping the world with worthless seedlings, which offer little that is unique, rare or useful is easy. Developing and identifying plants possessing the latter qualities should be the hybridizer's sole objective. In realizing this objective, there is no substitute for experience in getting rid of over 99% of your seedlings before they consume much energy or space. There may well be an element of lingering doubt, that a 'young dud' may turn out to be an attractive "senior citizen," but don't bet on it. Judging the potential of the very young, the spindly, when the seedlings bear their few leaves is far from a perfectly, rational process. The leaf-shape, texture, color pattern and distribution will change if the plant is given a chance to live.

As a hybridizer, you are judge, jury, forecaster as well as executioner, but ruthless purging of "unworthy" plants does not attach any social stigma to hybridizers. Your criteria of selection should be based on as much knowledge and experience as possible. You should have travelled enough and seen enough to know what already exists, what is already available in the market. The chances are that the breeding objective which you seek is something that you can claim as your own, a plant with a new combination of unique, rare and useful traits that can find a particular niche in the garden, or do a particular job very well. Obviously, the more you travel and look, the more likely you can avoid developing HYBRIDIZER'S MYOPIA, a commonplace affliction that has much in common with an overindulgent parent.

Rare traits are rare for good reason. Either the genes for the rare trait did not exist before, and the serendipitous mutation, or new gene occurred in your garden, with or without your help, possibly through the use of radiation or chemical mutagens. Further, rare genes tend to be "shy" in the company of those genes which control the more common plant traits, another way of saying that rare genes are recessive, relative to the dominant or common gene. Their presence is effectively masked, waiting for that set of circumstances when the dominant gene isn't on hand and thus able to express itself. The rare gene may also be "rare" because it depends on the cooperation of the right combination of several other genes. Helper genes which tend to be in a "switched-off" position may have to be "switched-on" before the "new kid" can come into being. The laws of probability are alive and well in the botanic world. The odds of developing a unique combination are working against you, even when the basic programming exists within every cell of the plants selected as parents. This game is for the long-term. Think in terms of decades, in terms of patience, good records, good observation and the wisdom to know what you have and what to do with it. You don't have to "beat the odds" to have some fun and a sense of well-being as an amateur. At least half of the fun is found in working with living plants with a plan in mind.

Hybridizer's myopia? *H.* 'Invincible' is sun-tolerant, pest-resistant, vigorous and heavily set with fragrant flowers.

The Hosta Book

XIV

PAUL ADEN

Recommendations for the Landscape

As learning has always been and remains essentially an individual matter, it should be clear that my recommendations of hostas for landscape use, is at least to a degree, subjective, and in any event, should not be considered a substitute for viewing mature clumps, or at least good color illustrations before you decide to use a particular hosta at a particular spot in your landscape. As this book is intended to be used as a reference tool by a variety of gardeners, the authors have endeavored to sustain a consistent standard of objectivity based on long-term, personal experience. I trust that most readers will concur that these recommendations reasonably approximate the best of the *Hosta* cultivars. My professional interest has, and continues to be based on the evaluation of plants in

The recommendations are based on long-term, personal experience.

twenty different genera, most of which have been sent to me by other people. In the course of this work, it has been my lot and good fortune to grow and evaluate all of the *Hosta* species and almost all of the noteworthy *Hosta* cultivars developed worldwide.

The criteria involved in the recommendations contained in this chapter are:

1. *Performance* under a wide range of home garden conditions

2. *Identifiable* without looking at a label at normal viewing distance and

3. *Class* or something you can enjoy and feel proud to live with.

The meaning of some of the information in the descriptions is as follows:

Number in (#) = # required/sq. yd. (multiply by 1.2 for # required/sq. meter).

EDGERS number in (#) = # required/running yd. (Multiply by 1.1 for # required/running meter).

SMALL—8 in. (20 cm) or less, suitable for rock garden or small garden settings;

EDGER—12 in. (30 cm) or less, vigorous horizontal growth; not stoloniferous.

GROUNDCOVER: 18 in. (45 cm) or less; reduces maintenance and binds soil.

BACKGROUND: Lush, architectural, 24 in. (60 cm) or taller can be used to increase privacy.

SPECIMEN: any size, site close to viewer to enjoy detail, texture, color pattern, buds, flower or fragrance.

119

H. **'Big Daddy'** Background; deep blue; round, very puckered leaves 9 in. (22½ cm) wide, 11 in. (27½ cm) long; dense mound 40 in. (100 cm) wide, 36 in. (90 cm) high; good substance; rapid grower; noted for its architectural "look;" makes a dramatic statement; pest-resistant; floriferous, lots of white flowers in early summer; shade to ¾ sun; (3)

H. **'Big Mama'** Background; intense blue hosta; excellent for screening and creating private spaces; large, cupped, puckered leaves 12 in. (30 cm) wide, 13 in. (32½ cm) long; mound 44 in. (110 cm) wide, 40 in. (100 cm) high; rapid-grower; floriferous; many early-summer scapes filled with lavender flowers; shade to ¾ sun; (3)

H. **'Blue Angel'** Background; blue; A novice seeing this plant as a mature clump in bloom for the first time could easily become a "hosta-believer"; huge, heavily-textured, very blue leaves, 12 in. (30 cm) wide, 16 in. (40 cm) long, create a lush, even tropical "look" in the garden; tiered mound 50 in. (125 cm) wide and 48 in. (120 cm) high; many white, hyacinth-like flowers for a long period in summer; effective in flower arrangements; shade to ¾ sun; (1)

H. **'Blue Mammoth'** Background; light-blue giant; leaves with heavy puckering 12 in. (30 cm) wide, 14 in. (35 cm) long, good substance and form; one of the largest hostas, mound 54 in. (135 cm) wide, 48 in. (120 cm) high; rapid grower; floriferous, lots of early, pale lavender flowers; excellent for screening; shade to ¾ sun; (1)

H. **'Blue Moon'** Small; blue; leaves with good substance, pest-resistant, 2 in. wide, 3 in. long; neat mound which grows in a flat clump 5 in. (12½ cm) high, 9 in. (22½ cm) wide; produces dense racemes of white flowers in late summer; best suited for rock garden or groundcover use; slug-resistant; shade to ¾ sun; (18)

H. **'Blue Umbrellas'** Background; blue to blue-green; leaves 10 in. (25 cm) wide, 12 in. (30 cm) long; dense, symmetrical mound 40 in. (100 cm) wide, 36 in. (90 cm) high; landscape "powerhouse"; looks great almost anywhere; leaves with heavy substance and texture; rapid grower; pest-resistant; sun-tolerant; excellent for screening; many lavender flowers edged in white; shade to full sun; (1)

H. **'Blue Wedgwood'** Edger; blue; from England; leaves 3 in. (7½ cm) wide, 7 in. (17½ cm) long; mound 12 in. (30 cm) wide, 10 in. (25 cm) high; equally useful as an edger or a groundcover; rapid grower; pale lavender blossoms in early summer; shade to ½ sun; (3)

H. **'Chartreuse Wiggles'** Small; chartreuse to gold; almost looks like an exotic sea animal; lance-shaped leaves ½ in. (1 cm) wide, 5 in. (12½ cm) long,

H. 'Big Daddy'

H. 'Big Mama'

H. 'Blue Umbrellas'

H. 'Blue Wedgwood'

H. 'Color Glory'

H. 'Excitation'

H. 'Fall Bouquet'

H. 'Fascination'

heavily ruffled; neat, low mound 3 in. (7½ cm) high, 10 in. (25 cm) wide; lavender flowers in late summer; small hosta award winner; shade to ¾ sun; (18)

***H.* 'Citation'** Specimen; variegated; white margin with chartreuse to gold centers; twisting leaves 3 in. (7½ cm) wide, 7 in. (17½ cm) long; flat mound 7 in. (17½ cm) high, 12 in. (30 cm) wide; looks like exotic jewelry or a lovely marine animal; beautiful buds; lots of pale lavender flowers midseason complements the foliage; shade to full sun; (16)

***H.* 'Color Glory'** Specimen; variegated; with yellow center and wide, irregular margin of blue and green tones of excellent stability; natural, variegated "sport" of *H. sieboldiana* 'Elegans'; leaves are round 8 in. (20 cm) wide, 9 in. (22½ cm) long, puckered with good substance; cascading mound 36 in. (90 cm) high, 40 in. (100 cm) wide; pest-resistant; sun-tolerant; quite vigorous, probably the best grower of the 'Elegans' sports; mound 30 in. (75 cm) high by 40 in. (100 cm.) wide; dense mass of white flowers in summer just above the foliage; shade to ¾ sun; (1)

***H.* 'Excitation'** Small; chartreuse to gold; gold sport of *H* 'Citation'; leaves 2½ in. (6 cm) wide, 6 in. (15 cm) long; tailored mound 6 in. (15 cm) high, 10 in. (25 cm) wide; useful in corsages and arrangements; many, pale orchid flowers in summer; shade to ¾ sun; (18)

***H.* 'Fall Bouquet'** Edger; dark green; leaves slightly wavy, pointed, 3 in. (7½ cm) wide, 8 in. (20 cm) long, held on red petioles, good substance; symmetrical, neat mound, 12 in. (30 cm) high, 18 in. (45 cm) wide; rapid grower; also useful as groundcover; quite suitable for flower arranging; floriferous, dense display of blue flowers in the fall; shade to full sun; (4)

***H.* 'Fascination'** Specimen; variegated; center of white, cream, yellow and chartreuse with wide, irregular margin made of shades of green; leaves 6 in. (15 cm) wide, 7 in. (17½ cm) long; mound 14 in. (35 cm) high, 20 in. (50 cm) wide; beautiful buds densely-packed; pale lavender flowers in midseason complement the foliage; useful in flower arrangements; ¼ to ¾ sun; (6)

***H. fluctuans* 'Variegated'** Background; variegated; frosted-green base with wide, irregular margins of bright yellow; leaves 8 in. (20 cm) wide, 9 in. (22½ cm) long twist, good substance; upright, vase-shaped mound 40 in. (100 cm) high, 36 in. (90 cm) wide; very effective on a slope; appreciated when mature; many pale-orchid flowers in midseason; shade to ¾ sun; (2)

***H.* 'Francee'** Groundcover; variegated; forest-green leaves with bright, white margins; leaves 5 in. (12½ cm) wide, 6 in. (15 cm) long; neat, but elegant mound 24 in. (60 cm) high, 30 in. (75 cm) wide; rapid grower; lavender flowers in late summer; large hosta award winner; shade to ¾ sun; (6)

H. 'Fragrant Bouquet' Specimen; variegated; apple-green base and wide, irregular, light yellow margin; broad leaves, 8 in. (20 cm) wide, 10 in. (25 cm) long, wavy with good substance; dense mound 18 in. (45 cm) high, 26 in. (65 cm) wide; rapid grower; pest-resistant; sun-tolerant; beautiful buds appear flower-like before opening; 32 in. scapes, some vestigial leaves; floriferous, many flat, out-facing, radially-arranged, white flowers, with light blue tinge (disappears during the day), typically 3–4 in. (7½–10 cm) across, and extremely fragrant, in mid-July and early August, tend to rebloom into the fall when established; flowers and foliage useful in flower arrangements; shade to ¾ sun; (2)

H. 'Frances Williams' Background; variegated; wide, yellow irregular margin, blue-green base; round, puckered leaves 8 in. (20 cm) wide, 10 in. (25 cm) long; cascading mound 32 in. (80 cm) high, 40 in. wide (100 cm); spectacular when mature; early-blooming, pale-lavender flowers; shade to ½ sun; (2)

H. 'Fringe Benefit' Background; variegated; green base and wide, white margins; heart-shaped leaves 7 in. (17½ cm) wide, 9 in. (22½ cm) long; dense mound 36 in. (90 cm) high, 42 in. (105 cm) wide; rapid grower; pest-resistant; versatile performer in the landscape; floriferous, pale lavender flowers in early summer; shade to full sun; (2)

H. 'Gaiety' Edger; variegated; yellow base which often shows a green midline, and a neat cream margin; leaves 3 in. (7½ cm) wide, 8 in. (20 cm) long, good substance; bright mound, 5 in. (12½ cm) high, 12 in. (30 cm) wide, tends to grow flat; rapid grower; pest-resistant; lots of pale orchid flowers in mid-summer; shade to ¾ sun; (5)

H. 'Gold Edger' Edger; chartreuse to gold; heart-shaped leaves 3 in. (7½ cm) wide, 4 in. (10 cm) long; neat, dense mound 10 in. (25 cm) high, 12 in. (30 cm) wide; rapid grower, adjacent mounds mesh quickly; sun-tolerant; pest-resistant; floriferous, masses of lavender flowers in midsummer; ½ to full sun; (4)

H. 'Francee'

H. 'Fragrant Bouquet'

H. 'Frances Williams'

H. 'Gold Edger'

H. 'Gold Standard'

H. 'Golden Tiara'

H. 'Grand Master'

H. 'Green Fountain'

H. **'Gold Standard'** Groundcover; variegated; yellow base, green margins; leaves 5 in. (12½ cm) wide, 7 in. (17½ cm) long; mound 24 in. (60 cm) high, 30 in. (75 cm) wide; rapid grower; best color when mature; pale lavender flowers in midseason; large hosta award winner; ¼ to ¾ sun; (6)

H. **'Golden Tiara'** Edger; variegated; light green base, yellow margins; sport of *H. nakaiana*; heart-shaped leaves 3 in. (7½ cm) wide, 4 in. (10 cm) long; mound 12 in. (30 cm) high, 16 in. (40 cm) wide; rapid grower; neat; purple flowers in midsummer; a small hosta award winner; shade to ¾ sun; (3)

H. gracillima 'Variegated' (*H. cathyana* 'Variegated') Groundcover; variegated; green base, cream margin; lance-shaped leaves ¾ in (2 cm) wide, 7 in. (17½ cm) long; neat, upright mound 8 in. (20 cm) high, 6 in. (15 cm) wide; stoloniferous; rapid grower; excellent on slopes, suitable for soil erosion control; lavender flowers in summer; shade to full sun; (10)

H. **'Grand Master'** Groundcover; variegated; blue-green base and white margin; much-improved *H.* 'Francee'; slightly wavy, heart-shaped, puckered leaves, 6 in. (15 cm) wide, 8 in. (20 cm) long; symmetrical mound 16 in. (40 cm) high, 22 in. (55 cm) wide; rapid grower; pest-resistant; sun-tolerant; 30 in. (75 cm) scape with vestigial leaves that appear flower-like at early stage; dense blue buds above mound appear flower-like before opening; floriferous, heavy display of blue flowers in summer; very suitable for bouquets; shade to full sun; (3)

H. **'Great Expectations'** Specimen; variegated; extremely wide, irregular margin of blue and green enveloping a light yellow-cream center; in terms of sheer beauty, the best, natural "sport" of *H. sieboldiana* 'Elegans' yet seen; discovered in a very long and very old line of hosta clumps; leaves round and puckered 8 in. (20 cm) wide, 8 in. (20 cm) long, good substance; mound 22 in. (55 cm) high, 30 in. (75 cm) wide; appears as a giant flower; floriferous, dense mass of white flowers in summer just above the foliage; keep this plant close to the viewer and give it space; shade to ¾ sun; (1)

H. **'Green Fountain'** Groundcover; green; lustrous green leaves 3 in. (7½ cm) wide, 10 in. (25 cm) long, cascade in a fountain-like display; mound 36 in. (90 cm) high, 32 in. (80 cm) wide; highly pest-resistant; set close to eye level on a slope; sun-tolerant; floriferous, bunches of lavender flowers in late summer; shade to full sun; (2)

H. **'Green Wedge'** Background; light green to gold; green changes to gold with more light; improved *H. nigrescens* 'Elatior'; huge, glossy, majestic leaves 10 in. (25 cm) wide, 12 in. (30 cm) long, heavy substance; mound 42 in. (105 cm) high, 48 in. (120 cm)

H. 'Green Wedge'

H. 'Janet'

H. 'Just So'

H. 'Lights Up'

wide; pest-resistant; sun-tolerant; floriferous, lots of lavender flowers in midsummer; shade to full sun; (1)

H. **'Ground Master'** Groundcover; variegated; green base, undulating white margin; leaves 4 in. (10 cm) wide, 10 in. (25 cm) long; mound 12 in. (30 cm) high, 16 in. (40 cm) wide; rapid grower; stoloniferous, excellent for controlling soil erosion and weed growth; floriferous, lots of lavender flowers in late summer; shade to ¾ sun; (9)

H. **'Hadspen Blue'** Groundcover; blue; from England; leaves with good form and substance 4 in. (10 cm) wide, 5 in. (12½ cm) long; mound 12 in. (30 cm) high, 16 in. (40 cm) wide; pest-resistant; many lavender flowers provide graceful contrast to blue foliage in late summer; shade to ¾ sun; (9)

H. **'Invincible'** Edger; bright, glossy green; leaves slightly wavy and pointed, 4 in. (10 cm) long, 2½ in. (6 cm) wide; mound 10 in. high, 12 in. (30 cm) wide, with leaves tightly-massed; pest-resistant; sun-tolerant; rapid grower; also useful as groundcover; floriferous, masses of densely-packed, fragrant, blue flowers for long period in summer; shade to full sun; (3)

H. **'Janet'** Groundcover; variegated; chameleon-like base color which varies from chartreuse to yellow to white as season progresses, offset with green margins; leaves 3 in. (7½ cm) wide, 10 in. (25 cm) long; mound 16 in. (40 cm) high, 20 in. (50 cm) wide; delicate, pale lavender flowers in late summer; shade to ¾ sun; (6)

H. **'Just So'** Small; variegated; blue-green margin and yellow center; leaves puckered, pointed, 2 in. (5 cm) wide, 5 in. (12½ cm) long; mound 3–4 in. (7½–10 cm) high, 8 in. (20 cm) wide; tends to be flat; pest-resistant; 12 in. (30 cm) scape; pink-lavender flowers in midsummer; shade to ¾ sun; (15)

H. **'Lights Up'** Small; yellow; leaves very wavy, upright, very early to emerge in spring; ¾ in. (2 cm) wide, 5 in. (12½ cm) long; upright mound 3½ in. (8½ cm) high, 4 in. (10 cm) wide; somewhat stoloniferous; rapid grower; scape 8 in. (20 cm) high; white-striped, purple flowers in summer; shade to ¾ sun; (80)

H. **'Little Aurora'** Small; gold; smallest *H. tokudama* offered; 2 in. (5 cm) wide, 3 in. (7½ cm) long leaves cupped, puckered, with metallic sheen; mound 6 in. (15 cm) high, 8 in. (20 cm) wide; rapid grower; also useful as edger; many pale lavender flowers in summer; ¼ to ¾ sun; (12)

H. **'Love Pat'** Specimen; blue; improved form of the species, *H. tokudama*, in size, vigor, color and versatility; 7 in. (17½ cm) wide, 8 in. (20 cm) long, leaves puckered, textured, with heavy substance; upright mound 22 in. (55 cm) high, 18 in. (45 cm)

wide; popular with flower arrangers; color holds up well in considerable sun; floriferous; many pale lavender flowers in early summer; shade to ¾ sun; (4)

H. 'Midas Touch' Groundcover; gold; round, cupped, heavily-puckered leaves 5 in. (12½ cm) wide, 6 in. (15 cm) long, with amazing texture, invites your touch; dramatic, somewhat upright, mound 14 in. (35 cm) wide, 20 in. (50 cm) high; great attention-getter; foliage complemented by pale lavender flowers in summer; ¼ to full sun; (6)

H. montana 'Aureo-marginata' Background; variegated; glossy green base, wide, irregular, yellow margins; huge leaves 12 in. (30 cm) wide, 14 in. (35 cm) long; spectacular when mature; very early to emerge in spring; mound 42 in. (105 cm) high, 48 in. (120 cm) wide; "specimen" quality, for sheer impact; allow space or smaller plants in surroundings; lots of pale-lavender flowers in early summer; shade to ¾ sun; (1)

H. 'On Stage' Specimen; variegated; 2-tone green margin and white center; from Japan; leaves, eventually get to 10 in. long and 6 in. wide; effective in flower arrangements; mound 14 in. high, 24 in. wide; particularly sun-proof; scape 24 in. (60 cm) high; trumpet-shaped, light blue flowers in summer; requires sun for best variegation; shade to full sun; (2)

H. 'Piedmont Gold' Background; gold; 5 in. (12½ cm) wide, 7 in. (17½ cm) long leaves with attractive, curved twist; mound 18 in. (45 cm) high, 24 in. (60 cm) wide; rapid grower; lots of white flowers in midsummer; winner of large hosta award; ¼ to ¾ sun; (3)

H. 'Pixie Power' Small; variegated; white base and green margins; ½ in. (1 cm) wide, 5 in. (12½ cm) long leaves; neat, tiny mounds 2 in. (5 cm) high, 5 in. (12½ cm) wide; midsummer lavender flowers; avoid strong afternoon sun; shade to ½ sun; (48)

H. 'Reversed' Specimen; variegated; cream centers set off by very wide, irregular margin of blue and green; 6 in. (15 cm) wide, 7 in. (17½ cm) long leaves of heavy substance; dense, symmetrical mound 16 in. (40 cm) high, 20 in. (50 cm) wide; one of the most beautiful hostas; the "opposite" of H. 'Frances Williams' with none of its faults; pest-resistant; attractive buds; floriferous, lavender flowers in summer; shade to ¾ sun; (6)

H. shaishu jima Small; green; ½ in. (1 cm) wide, 4 in. (10 cm) long leaves, spear-shaped, wavy margin, ½ in. wide, 4 in. (10 cm) long, good substance; neat mound, 3 in. (7½ cm) high, 6 in. (15 cm) wide; rapid grower; also good as low edger; 10 in. (25 cm) scape; purple flowers in midseason; shade to ¾ sun; (36)

H. 'Midas Touch

H. 'On Stage'

H. 'Piedmont Gold'

Recommendations for the Landscape

H. *shaishu jima* used as an edger.

H. 'Sea Drift'

H. 'Shade Fanfare'

H. 'Shade Master'

H. **'Sea Drift'** Background; green; leaves "piecrusted" 5 in. (12½ cm) wide, 7 in. (17½ cm) long; improved *H.* 'Green Piecrust'; mound 24 in. (60 cm) high, 30 in. (75 cm) wide; rapid grower; sun-tolerant; pest-resistant; lots of lavender-pink flowers in midseason; shade to full sun; (2)

H. **'Sea Sprite'** Small; variegated; yellow to cream base, wavy, green margins; leaves 1 in. (2½ cm) wide, 5 in. (12½ cm) long; 3 in. (7½ cm) high, 6 in. (15 cm) wide; mound low and flat; improvement on *H.* 'Kabitan' with greater pest-resistance and sun-tolerance; stoloniferous; rapid-grower; good on slopes; pale orchid flowers in midsummer; shade to ¾ sun; (18)

H. **'Shade Fanfare'** Groundcover; variegated; light green to gold center accented by broad, cream-colored margin; leaves 5 in. (12½ cm) wide, 7 in. (17½ cm) long; mound 18 in. (45 cm) high, 22 in. (55 cm) wide; rapid grower; pest-resistant; foliage color is best in more sun; beautiful buds; floriferous, lavender flowers in midsummer; shade to full sun; (6)

H. **'Shade Master'** Groundcover; gold; colors early, even in dark areas; leaves 6 in. (15 cm) wide, 8 in. (20 cm) long; mound 24 in. (60 cm) high, 30 in. (75 cm) wide; rapid grower; good weed control; "brightens" dark corners in garden; beautiful lavender flowers in midsummer; shade to ¾ sun; (6)

H. **'Shining Tot'** Small; deep green; dwarf *H. pulchella*-type; high lustre leaves ⅓ in. (1 cm) wide, 3 in. (7½ cm) long; very attractive mound 1 in. (2½ cm) high, 3 in. (7½ cm) wide; sun-tolerant; rapid grower; flower scape in scale with mound; lilac flowers in midsummer; shade to full sun; (36)

H. **'Shogun'** Background; variegated; blue-green base, very wide, irregular, white margins; leaves 8 in. (20 cm) wide, 10 in. (25 cm) long; upright mound 30 in. (75 cm) high, 24 in. (60 cm) wide; effective with bold companion plants; rapid grower; many scapes of pale orchid flowers for late summer bouquets; shade to ¾ sun; (1)

The Hosta Book

H. **'So Sweet'** Specimen; variegated; wide, white margin on green base; glossy leaves 7 in. (17½ cm) long, 4½ in. (11 cm) wide; mound 14 in. (35 cm) high, 20 in. (50 cm) wide; 25 in. (62.5 cm) scape; floriferous, large, white, fragrant flowers in August; shade to ¾ sun; (3)

H. **'Spritzer'** Specimen; variegated; rippling, green margin and yellow to white center; pointed leaves 10 in. (25 cm) long, 2½ in (6 cm) wide; upright mound 18 in. (45 cm) high, 14 in. (35 cm) wide; site on slope to enjoy form; pest-resistant; sun-tolerant; 28 in. (70 cm) scape; floriferous, light blue, horn-shaped flowers in summer; shade to full sun; (4)

H. **'Squiggles'** Small; variegated; cream base with irregular, two-tone, green margins; twisting leaves 1 in. (2½ cm) wide, 4 in. (10 cm) long; unique, pinwheel-shaped mound 4 in. (10 cm) high, 8 in. (20 cm) wide; bright white flowers in midsummer, shade to ¾ sun; (36)

H. **'Sum and Substance'** Background; chartreuse to gold (varies with light); large, glossy, tough, textured leaves 9 in (22½ cm) wide, 10 in. (25 cm) long, with substance that must be felt to be believed; upright mound 30 in. (75 cm) high, 24 in. (60 cm) wide; extra effective on a slope, takes full sun in Alabama; very pest-resistant; lots of lavender flowers in late summer; large hosta award winner; ¼ to full sun; (3)

H. **'Sun Power'** Background; gold; distinctive, twisting, leaves 5 in. (12½ cm) wide, 10 in. (25 cm) long; mound 30 in. (75 cm) high, 36 in. (90 cm) wide; colors early and keep color until frost, even in the shade; rapid grower; floriferous; light orchid flowers in midseason offset the unique gold foliage; shade to ¾ sun; (1)

H. tardiflora Edger; dark green; choice, delightful species; leaves 1½ in. (3½ cm) wide, 6 in. (15 cm) long, lance-shaped, neat, lustrous leaves, red petioles, good substance; neat, symmetrical mound 10 in. (25 cm) high, 12 in. (30 cm) wide; rapid grower; dense display of lavender flowers for long period in the fall; shade to full sun; (4)

H. **'Thumb Nail'** Small; frosted green; smallest *H. venusta*-type seen yet; leaves ½ in. (1 cm) wide, 1 in. (2½ cm) long; mound 2 in. (5 cm) high, 4 in. (10 cm) wide; rapid grower; stoloniferous, effective in controlling soil erosion; lilac flowers in midsummer; shade to ¾ sun; (56)

H. tokudama 'Aureo-nebulosa' Specimen; variegated; center suffused with yellow, wide, irregular margins in shades of blue and green; choice species; leaves 4 in. (10 cm) wide, 4 in. (10 cm) long, round, cupped, heavily-puckered, good substance; mound 12 in. (30 cm) high, 16 in. (40 cm) wide; slow grower; beautiful, white flowers in early summer; shade to ½ sun; (9)

H. 'So Sweet'

H. 'Spritzer'

H. 'Squiggles'. Note how the color of the nearby blue seedling "works" well with the white center of *H.* 'Squiggles'.

H. tortifrons Specimen; green; unique, attractive species; ½ in. wide, 7 in. long leaves thinner than *H. tardiflora*, that twist and turn, almost whimsical; upright mound 8 in. (20 cm) wide, 6 in. (15 cm) wide; choice in rock garden; heavy flowering with lilac racemes for a long period in the fall; shade to full sun; (36)

H. 'Sun Power' (C. Allen. Courtesy of Klehm Nursery)

H. **'True Blue'** Background; blue; heavy-textured, puckered leaves 7 in. (17½ cm) wide, 8 in. (20 cm) long; mound 24 in. (60 cm) high, 30 in. (75 cm) wide; color holds for long time, even in considerable sun; large flared mound; pest-resistant; lots of unusual orchid flowers edged in white in midseason; ¼ to¾ sun; (3)

H. **'Vanilla Cream'** Edger; chartreuse to gold to cream; heavily-substanced leaves 2 in. (5 cm) wide, 2 in. (5 cm) long; 5 in. (12½ cm) high, 8 in. (20 cm) wide; neat, unique, flat-growing mound; pest-resistant; many lavender flowers in summer; ½ to full sun; (6)

H. venusta 'Variegated'

H. 'True Blue'

H. 'White Colossus'

The Hosta Book

H. ventricosa 'Aureo-marginata' Groundcover; specimen; superb species; variegated; dark green base, unique twisting, broad, irregular margin of yellow that turns to white; large, heart-shaped leaves 7 in. (17½ cm) wide, 8 in. (20 cm) long; mound 24 in. (60 cm) high, 30 in. (75 cm) wide; mauve flowers in midseason; shade to ¾ sun; (6)

H. venusta 'Variegated' Small; variegated; cream center and two-tone, wavy, green margins; leaves ½ in. (1 cm) wide, 4 in. (10 cm) long; mound 3–4 in. (7½–10 cm) high, 6 in. (15 cm) wide; vigorous despite reduced number of chlorophyll cells; stoloniferous; good pot plant; very effective with "blues" in shady areas; lavender flowers in midseason; shade to ¾ sun; (36)

H. 'White Colossus' Specimen; variegated; initial leaf-center of chartreuse which turns white, margin in shades of green; leaves 5 in. (12½ cm) wide, 10 in. (25 cm) long; mound 14 in. (35 cm) wide, 22 in. (55 cm) wide; effective with "blues" in the shade; slow grower; foliage quite suitable for flower arranging; light orchid flowers in midsummer; shade to ½ sun; (5)

H. 'White Magic' Specimen; variegated; center of white offset by wide, irregular margins of green and gold; leaves 5 in. (12½ cm) wide, 6 in. (15 cm) long; mound 14 in. (35 cm) high, 20 in. (50 cm) wide; stops you in your tracks when mature; very effective when grouped with blues in shady areas; beautiful buds; lots of pale lavender flowers in midseason; shade to ½ sun; (9)

H. 'Wide Brim' Specimen; variegated; blue-green center and very wide, irregular margins of cream with gold tints at maturity; leaves 6 in. (15 cm) wide, 8 in. (20 cm) long; mound 18 in. (45 cm) high, 24 in. (60 cm) wide; rapid grower; attractive buds; lots of dense, pale lavender flower heads in summer; very popular with flower arrangers; shade to ¾ sun; (6)

H. 'Zounds' Background; metallic gold; glossy, puckered 7 in. (17½ cm) wide, 8 in. (20 cm) long leaves, seem to glow, particularly at dusk; mound 22 in. (55 cm) high, 26 in. (65 cm) wide; livens up dark areas; pale lavender flowers in midseason nicely offset golden foliage; ¼ to ¾ sun; (3)

A view of the Garden of Aden. (C. Allen. Courtesy of Klehm Nursery)

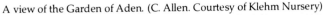

Recommendations for the Landscape

Appendix

Retail Nursery Sources were chosen not only on the quality of reputation in delivering a variety of choice perennial plants (including hostas), and serving their customers, but who also produced catalogs with good descriptions (and illustrations) that made intelligent consumer choices more probable. Those nurseries that ship MAIL-ORDER will be noted with (MO). For customers in foreign countries, it is wise to write ahead to determine limitations on foreign shipments. With the high cost of printing catalogs, it is fair to assume that there is a charge for catalogs, often deducted from the first order.

UNITED STATES:

KLEHM NURSERY (MO)
Route 5, Box 197
South Barrington, IL 60010

WAYSIDE GARDENS (MO)
Hodges, SC 29695

ANDRE VIETTE NURSERIES (MO)
Route 1, Box 6
Fisherville, VA 22939

ENGLAND:

BRESSINGHAM NURSERIES (MO)
Bressingham, Diss, Norfolk
1P22 2AB ENGLAND

UNUSUAL PLANTS (MO)
White Bam House, Elmstead Market
Colchester, Essex CO7 7DB
ENGLAND

GERMANY:

HEINZ KLOSE (MO)
3503 Lohfelden bei Kassel
Rosenstrasse 10
WEST GERMANY

JAPAN:

HIROO ISHIGURO
Kami-Marubuchi,
Sofue Cho, Nakajima
Aichi Pref. JAPAN

KAMO NURSERIES
Harasato, Kakegawa,
Shizuoka 436-01 JAPAN

KOGORO SUZUKI
2222, Tomioka-machi,
Kanazawa-ku
Yokohama, JAPAN

KENJI WATANABE
59-1 Nagatsuka, Gotemba-shi
Shizuoka-Ken, Japan 412

Index

131